W9-ANN-832

ENGLISH MARKET TOWNS

A flower seller in Barnard Castle's market place, which boasts a superb Market Cross. Dating from the eighteenth century, it reflects the town's past prosperity.

ENGLISH MARKET TOWNS

RUSSELL CHAMBERLIN

HARMONY BOOKS

NEW YORK

A fourteenth-century misericord from Ludlow Church showing 'the successful townsman'. The flitcher indicates affluence.

Endpapers : Chipping Campden market hall.

Copyright © 1985 by Russell Chamberlin

All rights reserved. No part of this book may be reproduced or transmitted in any form or by any means, electronic or mechanical, including photocopying, recording, or by any information storage and retrieval system, without permission in writing from the publisher.

Published in the United States in 1985 by Harmony Books, a division of Crown Publishers, Inc., One Park Avenue, New York, New York 10016.

HARMONY and colophon are trademarks of Crown Publishers, Inc.

Published originally in Great Britain by George Weidenfeld and Nicolson, 91 Clapham High Street, London SW4 7TA, England

Manufactured in Italy

Library of Congress Cataloging in Publication Data

Chamberlin, E. R. (Eric Russell), 1926-
    English market towns.

    Includes index.
1. England – Description and travel – 1971-   – Guide-books.   2. Market towns – England – Guide-books.   I. Title.
DA650.C44   1985   914.2'04858   84-15797

ISBN 0-517-55670-7

10 9 8 7 6 5 4 3 2 1

First American Edition

CONTENTS

THE EASTERN COUNTIES

THE NORTH

THE BORDERS

Berwick-on-Tweed

Hexham
Durham
Keswick
Appleby
Barnard Castle
Kendal
Richmond

Ripon

Skipton *Beverley*

Knutsford *Buxton* Louth
Bakewell

Newark-on-Trent
Grantham Boston

Melton Mowbray Spalding **King's Lynn**
Lichfield Stamford
Market Harborough Wymondham
Ludlow *Oundle* *Ely* *Beccles*
Huntingdon
Warwick *Bury St Edmunds*
Stratford-upon-Avon
Ledbury *Chipping Campden* *Ampthill* Saffron Walden
Ross-on-Wye Moreton-in-Marsh Thaxted
Stow-on-the-Wold *Hertford*
Cirencester Amersham Maldon
Abingdon
Chepstow Faringdon *Henley-on-Thames*
Marshfield *Windsor*
Chippenham *Newbury*
Bradford-on-Avon
Wells Frome Farnham
Glastonbury *Alton* *Godalming*
Barnstaple Shepton Mallet Hythe
Shaftesbury Rye
Blandford Forum *Chichester* Lewes
Okehampton
Newport
Bodmin
Totnes
Penzance
Helston Falmouth

INTRODUCTION

In one sense, the term 'market town' is all but tautological when applied to the historic towns of England for they all gained a substantial part of their income from trading. Archaeologists, indeed, use evidence of trading activity as one of the vital criteria in deciding whether a given community was urban or rural.

The word 'market', however, does have a precise historical significance. It is the concession granted, by the lord of the manor, to a community permitting 'the meeting together of people for the purchase and sale of provisions or live stock, publicly exposed, at a fixed time and place'. The market was valuable to the community, providing it with a means of disposing of surplus products, and drawing in trade from the surrounding countryside. It was valuable to the lord of the manor, who gained a substantial addition to his income by levying tolls on the traders. But the concession was by no means automatically granted and obtained. The king had to be convinced that a new market was needed in the locality and, in general, permission would not be granted unless the nearest market was more than 6 miles away.

Trading 'at a fixed time and place': this was the vital definition of a market which, in due course, was to have so much effect upon the physical shape of English towns. The market was expected to take place at least once a week in a public place known to all. The vast majority of them began outside the church door, the most obvious and best-known of all public places. Many, indeed, occurred inside the church itself, but from the thirteenth century onwards a sense of piety, combined with the practical desire to control the expanding market, dictated its removal to a secular site. Common sense, again, prescribed the best-known locality – usually the meeting place of a network of roads. The market did, however, bring with it from the church the most potent symbol of Christianity – the cross. Two illiterate traders sealing a bargain with a handclasp under the cross would regard that as inviolable an act as two businessmen today would regard their signatures on a contract.

The cross moved with the market. Most market crosses retained their simplicity of form – the one at Grantham is an excellent example of this. Elsewhere this image developed over the centuries into an elaborate structure, still known as 'the market cross' but capable now of sheltering certain classes of merchandise and their traders. Some developed into superb works of art, like that at Chichester, and even evolved into the local town hall: the 'crosses' at Wymondham and Barnard Castle both have upper chambers used as council rooms.

Meanwhile, the traders were moving in and setting up their stalls around the cross. These stalls, or shambles, could be heavy and solid like that surviving at Shepton Mallet, or a flimsy temporary structure. In either case, it was much easier for the stall holder to leave it set up, rather than to dismantle it at the end of the trading session. From the beginning there were running battles between the traders and the steward of the market place, the former attempting to leave his stall up permanently, the latter attempting to ensure its removal. Usually, the steward won. But sometimes the stall holder was victorious: his stall would remain up first by the week, then by the month, then indefinitely. Eventually, he or his successor on the site would be successful in turning it into a permanent building, creating a market 'encroachment'. These encroachments are very noticeable on a town plan in the form of little lanes on the edge of the market place: Ludlow in Shropshire and Skipton in Yorkshire are two of many towns with such evidence of long-forgotten arguments.

The 'market place' is often an idea more than an actual location in the Continental sense. Markets founded by monastics (and these unworldly men were remarkably adept at founding these very worldly organizations) were usually placed outside the main gate of the monastery, as at Glastonbury, or the cathedral, as at Wells. East Anglian towns tended to favour something along the lines of the Continental *place* or *piazza* or *platz*, that is, a formal site, usually fairly regular in shape and specifically set aside for the market. The great Tuesday Market Place in King's Lynn is an excellent example of this. But, in general, the English with their preference for ad hoc, rule of thumb arrangements preferred to adapt the High Street into a market place: towns as far apart as Frome in Somerset and Appleby in Cumbria well illustrate this tendency. Again, a town plan will show this clearly, the country road entering the town widening out to form the market place, then narrowing beyond.

Strictly speaking, the present-day supermarket and hypermarket and the so-called 'shopping centre' are lineal descendants of the market, expressed in modern terms. But apart from their claustrophobic atmosphere with artificial light and recycled air, these modern 'markets' are overwhelmingly different from their predecessors in that they form

The Market Cross at Wymondham in Norfolk houses a meeting place on the upper floor, an example of the evolution of the cross from its original simple form.

*At the heart of Cirencester the market square, like the
Roman forum, still performs its role as a meeting place.*

deliberately intended permanent structures. And the essence of the market place is the physical impermanence of the traders' stalls.

We take the survival of the market for granted but, looked at in anthropological terms, it is a truly remarkable example of a human activity transcending centuries of drastic social, economic and technological change. The original rights of the lord of the manor have long since been ceded to the local authority, but the market still operates, two or three times a week, drawing together people from miles around to the self same spot as that used by their ancestors from time immemorial.

Why do street markets survive in the modern world? The economic argument, from the point of view of the trader, is the most powerful. The rent for a stall (or rather for its site) varies widely around the country, ranging from about £4 a day in Lincolnshire to about £12 a day in Surrey. Rent and rates for a shop would be at least four times as much, without taking overheads into consideration.

But far more important than the actual cost of a stall is the fact that the stall holder, unlike the shop keeper, has an active market. He does not have to sit in an empty premises on a Monday morning, waiting for custom while rent, rates, electricity and water bills inexorably accumulate. The stall holder goes to where the people are expected to congregate. Many owners, indeed, will not only travel from market to market, but may very well own half a dozen different stalls in different market towns, usually all run by members of the same family, or by close associates. All in all, for economic reasons, it is understandable why stall holders accept the uncertainty of tenure and the very considerable physical discomforts.

The reasons why shoppers patronize an open market is not so obvious. Fruit, vegetables and flowers – the mainstay of most small-town markets – will perhaps be a little fresher and, probably, cheaper than that available in shops. But the difference is certainly not so great as to constitute the major attraction of the market. Much of the non-perishable goods for sale will be cheap, mass-produced items – plastic toys, gaudy glass objects, cut-price clothing. On a warm summer's day, it is

Richmond, Yorkshire, an example of a market place that has been specifically designed and set on one side to fulfill its commercial and social purpose.

obviously more appealing to do one's shopping in the open than in a crowded, stuffy shop. But the market will be as heavily patronized on a bleak January day as on a smiling June morning. All in all, the attraction of a market place seems, to a large extent, atavistic.

The market today would be immediately recognizable to a Saxon or Norman citizen of the town. The fair, by contrast, has changed entirely in its nature and purpose. When a town gained a charter permitting it to hold a market once a week or more, it might also gain the right to hold a fair once a year, usually on its patron saint's day. Fairs were markets on a larger scale, usually specializing in some produce. Although the majority were only of local importance, a fair conferred prestige upon the town. A few achieved national, and even international significance: in England, perhaps the most famous of all is St Bartholomew's in Smithfield, London, which provided a model both for *Bartholomew Fayre* by Ben Jonson and John Bunyan's *Pilgrim's Progress*. Among smaller fairs of national significance was that of St Botolph in Boston (see p. 84).

The hard core of the fair would be trade, but there would also be a carnival element, with entertainers attracted to the fair by the swollen numbers of people, freer with their money in this holiday atmosphere than usual. General or trade fairs continued until well into the nineteenth century, but gradually the purely trading factor lost ground to that of recreation and the fair today is simply an extremely noisy means of mechanical entertainment. Nevertheless, it is usually held on the same spot and with the same rights as conferred by medieval charter upon its ancient predecessors.

Fairs, and to a lesser extent markets, automatically attracted trouble-makers, and even well-conducted fairs and markets would produce arguments over rights between the various participants. It was in order to adjudicate these differences, and to punish wrong-doers, that a species of semi-autonomous court came into being. It was known colloquially as the Court of Pie Powder. The odd name is probably a corruption of the French *piedspoudres* ('dusty feet'), supposedly the condition of those who had walked miles to attend the event.

Once a year, in May, Boston's market place is given over to a major fair, St Botolph's Fair. This view shows the fair that took place in 1912.

Apart from their historic interest, and the fact that they possess (or once possessed) a market, the fifty towns in the present book have one factor in common: their population is 35,000 or less. This upper limit was adopted with very great reluctance for it automatically excluded some of the jewels of English culture. York, Norwich, Lincoln, Shrewsbury, Chester, Exeter – these and a score of other superb communities, all of which gave shelter to one or more thriving markets, were excluded on a question of size. They exceeded the admittedly arbitrary level of 35,000.

For population size has an immense significance in determining the character of a community. Until the nineteenth century, evidence of population growth was also evidence of urban health. Declining, or even static population figures were sure evidence of urban ill-health. Today, alas, the reverse is likely to be true. A sudden boom in population, together with its inevitable suburban sprawl, usually means that some wholly extraneous growth has been grafted onto the town. And even when the growth is 'natural' (that is, produced out of the community's own vitality like the light engineering works in Norwich or the food processing industry in York) it still obscures much of the community's traditional pattern. There is no disputing that 'market day' is a lively social event in these historic cities. But it tends to be an additional bonus, with the life of the city going on regardless of whether or not the market place is empty.

The ebb and flow of traditional market-town life can be detected more clearly in communities of 35,000 and less. Over 2000 years ago Plato argued in *The Republic* that the ideal size of a community is around 10,000. One of the remarkable aspects discovered during research for the present book is how many English market towns, flourishing in the liveliest possible manner, can be accommodated well within Plato's figure even now, the last quarter of the twentieth century: Ludlow in Shropshire (population 7579), the exquisite little city of Wells in Somerset (population 8374) and Barnard Castle in Co. Durham (population 5016) all bear testimony to the fact that it is not necessary to herd human beings together in their tens and hundreds of thousands in order to enjoy a balanced social and economic life.

Such smaller towns, however, tend to be located in relatively remote parts of the country and it is the intention of this book to give as wide a geographical coverage as possible. To that end, the towns are arranged in six regions, fifty being given fuller treatment in the main body of the text while a further twenty-five are given gazetteer references in an appendix.

Even the elementary act of classification into regions demonstrates the extraordinary diversity of towns that exist in England. Within the regions there are certain basic 'family' characteristics, but also endless variety: the towns of Wells and Shepton Mallet in Somerset, for example, are little more than 10 miles apart, but the one has all the dignity of a city, with its enormous cathedral and great inns lining a handsome market place, while the other is indubitably a small country town.

No distinction has been made between 'town' and 'city' so that side by side appear the 'city' of Wells (population 8374) and the 'town' of Boston (population 26,425). The English, and their mentors the French, are among the few Europeans who struggle to make some distinction between 'village', 'town' and 'city'. There is, in fact, no legal, workable or even meaningful distinction between the terms 'town' and 'city'. Indeed, there exists a widespread belief that at a certain population level and, in particular, with the possession of a cathedral, a community is automatically entitled to call itself a city. This is quite erroneous. As it happens, all cities have cathedrals but cathedrals are by no means always in cities, and many a giant urban community is obliged to content itself with the title of 'borough' while its tiny neighbour calls itself a 'city'. It requires an Order in Council, on petition to the monarch, for the upgrading of a community to be granted, a privilege bestowed with increasing reluctance as our towns get even bigger. So, in these pages, 'town' and 'city' quite legitimately appear as interchangeable definitions.

In contrast to the traditional market, the modern supermarket presents a very different front.

The pace of change has struck our market towns as with all other institutions. Over the past few years the cattle market has been banished to the outskirts of most towns. All too often the market place is now some dreary anonymous asphalt area from which cars are temporarily removed while, ironically, the traditional market place is wholly submerged in traffic as in Glastonbury. In some towns the market has been killed off altogether. Two cases in point are Chepstow – its very name means 'market place' – and Falmouth, which virtually came into being as a market place for pirates but whose citizens now have to go to Truro to find an open-air market. Nevertheless, towns like these have been included, for the market forces that created them have left their ineradicable physical imprint upon them.

It seems, indeed, that the market impulse is not only as old as civilization, but is seemingly indestructible. Even as we lament the metamorphosis of the traditional market place into dead, soulless, mechanical supermarkets and hypermarkets so, quite unheralded, has developed the 'craft market' – a little self-conscious, it is true, uncertain of its tenure and its direction, but a living growth of that most ancient custom.

In the following entries, place-name meanings are followed by their derivations, and population figures are based on 1984 estimates.

THE WEST COUNTRY

BARNSTAPLE. DEVON

'Bearda's post' *Anglo-Saxon*
Population: 19,025 *Market:* Tuesday, Friday

THE odd derivation of the town's name simply refers to the fact that a Saxon called Bearda had a boundary post or stone hereabouts. More importantly, that far greater Saxon, Alfred, established here one of his vital burhs or strongholds against the Danes. Some of the burhs simply disappeared after the military threat, others shrank into villages, some developed into towns. A generation after Alfred's death the burh at Bearda's post was evidently well established enough to receive a charter from Alfred's grandson, 'Athelstan, king, lord of eorls'. Granted in AD 930, this charter is the basis of Barnstaple's claim to be the oldest borough in England.

Among the privileges granted by Athelstan was the right to hold markets and fairs. Both flourish a thousand years later. The Pannier Market is held in a fascinating Victorian building which links the

Queen Anne's Walk. This beautiful building was the Exchange of the Barnstaple Merchant Venturers. The statue on the colonnade is of Good Queen Anne herself.

Guildhall in the High Street with the Queen's Hall in Boutport Street. The three-day fair is held in September and its opening at noon on the first Wednesday after 20 September is marked by a ceremony in the Guildhall. The town's splendid plate is laid out, and the mayor toasts the fair's success in spiced ale, made according to an Elizabethan recipe and served by the beadle in silver loving cups. This event retains a curious dignity, reflecting the very real social and economic role that the fair still plays in the life of north Devon's major market town.

For some 300 years, from the fourteenth to the sixteenth century, Barnstaple's prosperity was founded upon the sea. Both as shipbuilder and as port, the town dominated the north coast of Devon, gaining access to the Atlantic via the River Taw. But though the river brought wealth, it also formed a barrier and the first recorded attempt to bridge it took place in 1273. With justifiable pride, the town's records note how they thus tamed 'the great, huge, mighty, perylous and dreadful water named *Taw*'. (Self-abasement has never been a Devonian characteristic.) One of the features of this first bridge was a chantry chapel, built by the lord of Barnstaple, Henry de Tracey, in expiation of his uncle's crime in taking part in the murder of Thomas à Becket. The present bridge was built in 1347 and the incredible succession of arches – no less than sixteen – reflect the financial and engineering problems that were solved so remarkably by this small town.

The hand of the 'developer' has been laid fairly heavily on Barnstaple, but the heart of the town is still sound. It is an aesthetic delight of a high order to cross the Long Bridge from the delightfully named Sticklepath, walking high over the water to the dignified open space known simply as The Square. From there two streets follow the original boundaries of the town: the Strand (later becoming

The Pannier Market. This handsome iron-framed Victorian survival has been superbly restored and is again immensely popular as a market hall.

Castle Street), following the river bank and quay in a straight line and, curved from it like a bow, Boutport Street. The High Street intersects this approximate ellipse which enfolds the charming tangle of small streets that forms the heart of Barnstaple. Among them is Butcher's Row, a line of small, identical shops which are not only of very considerable architectural interest, but are also economically viable – an unusual combination of interests. Near the quay is the elegant colonnaded Queen Anne's Walk, with the Tome Stone on which merchants laid their money to seal a bargain. The old Guildhall was demolished in 1827 but the parlour of the present Guildhall holds a gem in the form of the seventeenth-century oak panelling which came from one of the town houses of a prosperous Barnstaple merchant. The Parish Church of St Peter, immediately identifiable by its twisted spire reminiscent of Chesterfield's, is mainly fourteenth century, the north and south aisles being added three centuries later – a tranquil oasis in the midst of Barnstaple's busy streets.

St Peter's Church. Its twisted spire, a local landmark, is reminiscent of Chesterfield's. The main body of the church is fourteenth century.

BRADFORD-ON-AVON, WILTSHIRE

'Broad ford on the river' Anglo-Saxon
Population: 8752 Market: occasional

A BEAUTIFUL bridge with one of the rare surviving bridge chapels; a tiny Saxon church which is probably the oldest Christian place of worship in England; a great tithe barn, larger than many a parish church – these three structures alone would give distinction to any town. And they form only part of Bradford's fabric. There cannot be many other towns in England where the principal industrial area is also part of the historic setting. The cloth mills that brought wealth to the town in the eighteenth century, and went into decline when the woollen trade collapsed, have been restored by the Avon Rubber Company. These buildings, in the beautiful honey-coloured stone typical of the West Country, form a typical backdrop to the river, but also contribute substantially to the economic life of the town. There is a scattering throughout the centre of antique shops and good, if expensive, restaurants catering for the crowds who come to visit what has been described as 'one of the most beautiful towns in England'. But a diversity of light industry (the revolutionary Moulton Bicycle was first built here) and new housing estates, tucked away from the historic centre, have brought new life to the town.

Human beings have been living on this spot, on

One of the two oldest Saxon churches in England, the Church of St Laurence was virtually discovered in 1856 after being used for other purposes.

the bend of the tranquil River Avon beneath the great cliff now known as 'Tory', for at least two and a half millenia. (The word itself has no political significance, deriving from the Anglo-Saxon word tor, or high hill.) The Saxons established themselves here sometime before AD 652 (a date based on a known Saxon civil war hereabouts) and by the turn of the century a daughter house to Malmesbury Abbey had been founded here. Most of the monastery had disappeared by the twelfth century, but the church survived. Its subsequent history is little short of remarkable. Most Saxon churches expanded unrecognizably during the spate of building and rebuilding after the Norman Conquest. The Church of St Laurence survived this period but, over the following centuries, virtually disappeared from sight for it was divided into two, used as a residential house and hemmed in by buildings. It was not until 1856 that the vicar of the parish church deduced the ecclesiastical origins of this ancient structure and, over the next half century or so, it was painstakingly restored. Today it remains one of only two unchanged Saxon churches in the country.

And, as though one such discovery in the town were not enough, in 1869 a local citizen bought the ruins of what appeared to be an eighteenth-century cloth factory high up on the Tory. Historical investigation showed that these were the ruins of a most ancient hermitage chapel, old when the Tudor topographer John Leland came to the town in 1553 and identified it. The chapel was restored and reconsecrated in 1871. It now stands among mellow private houses, all clinging to this steep hill at the end of a meandering upward path, from which superb views of the town below and the country beyond can be gained.

The 'broad ford over the river' inevitably led to the birth of a bridge at or near the same spot. The bridge as it stands is a product of seven centuries' development, from the thirteenth century (two arches survive from the first pack bridge) down to today. The chapel on the bridge became in due course the town lock-up, and even now there are iron bedsteads clamped to the interior walls. Overhead is a handsome weathervane in the form of a fish

– the Bradford gudgeon – which gave rise to a local epigram in which prisoners in the chapel were described as being 'over the water and under the fish'.

English towns tend to ignore their rivers and, even when the river is incorporated into the townscape, the further bank tends to be neglected. Bradford is most unusual in giving equal treatment to both sides. Indeed, it is on the far side that the great tithe barn is to be found. This superb fourteenth-century building fulfilled an economic function for the medieval church, for through it passed the taxes or tithes that contributed to the upkeep of Shaftesbury Abbey. Close by the bridge is a beautifully balanced 'bridgehead' with buildings from the fifteenth century onwards creating an unplanned square linked to a riverside garden, unfortunately bisected by a main road.

The bridge takes the traveller immediately into the very heart of the town. Despite its centuries-old existence, Bradford still bears clear evidence of its original topography for the church that lies to the west, the inns, shops and houses that cluster around Market Street still occupy what flat ground remains. Almost immediately, the road begins to climb the steep hill that first attracted dwellers to this place.

One of the few surviving bridge chapels in England, later converted into a lock-up. The weathervane is in the form of the Bradford gudgeon.

The tithe barn. Dating from the fourteenth century the barn acted as a collecting station for the great abbey of Shaftesbury.

FALMOUTH, CORNWALL

'Mouth of the River Fal' *Anglo-Saxon*
Population : 18,525 *Market :* suspended

THE Romans and Phoenicians knew Falmouth harbour. Genoese navigators had observed the odd shape of the headland behind the town and noted it down in their portolan charts. Spanish and French men-of-war used the harbour during their running battles of 1538. There are said to be only two other harbours to compare with this incomparable sweep of bays and headlands – the harbours of Rio de Janiero and Sydney. But whereas these became the sites of large cities as their countries began to be developed, Falmouth remained surrounded by open country for centuries after the harbour had become familiar to seamen. Henry VIII built mass-ive forts on the headlands at St Mawes and Pendennis to guard the Carrick Roads. Walter Raleigh, who of all people knew a good harbour when he saw one, described Falmouth as 'a havyn very notable and famous, and in a manner ye principal towne of all England'. He and Sir John Killigrew, governor of Pendennis Castle, petitioned James I to build a few houses for seafarers here. Despite pressure from neighbouring towns, James not only agreed to that, but also to the transference of the customs house from Truro to the still unnamed 'new town', a logical move which profoundly irritated the people of Truro. But it was not until 1660 that the new

Pendennis Castle. Sir John Killigrew, founder of Falmouth, not only used this castle as a base but frequently as a storehouse for piratical booty.

The Fal estuary with its parish church. The immense harbour, with its numerous inlets, has been compared with that of Sydney and Rio de Janeiro.

community had a name when Charles II decreed that it should be called Falmouth.

Killigrew was undoubtedly the true founder of the town. His family came to the area in 1385, and seems to have followed the trades of piracy, agriculture or trade with fine impartiality: Sir John actually used Pendennis Castle as a storehouse for booty, entering into agreement with local pirates to turn a blind eye to their presence in the haven in return for a cut of their loot. His family home, known as

Carefully preserved, the figureheads adorning one of Falmouth's 'opes' are reminiscent of the period when the 'wooden walls of England' brought wealth to the town.

Arwenack House, still survives and has the unusual distinction of being older than the town in which it is situated.

Under this energetic, if thoroughly unscrupulous man the new town grew swiftly. By the end of the 1660s its population was over a thousand, and the Killigrews became rich from market and fair dues which the Jacobean charter had granted them. Then, in 1670, Killigrew built the first quay and inaugurated what was to be Falmouth's most lucrative trade, and England's most remarkable service – the packet ships. Lightly armed and very fast, these ships' prime task was the transportation of mails, but they also carried bullion and important (and wealthy) passengers. They were the natural prey of pirates and privateers but though they could fight if necessary, their captains were under the strictest orders always to run rather than fight and, if capture became inevitable, to drop the mails in weighted packages. They achieved an incredible record: the West India packet service, for instance, ran for 200 years without a break, the boat leaving once a month and carrying about 1500 letters as well as one or two passengers. During the Napoleonic Wars they fought thirty-two engagements, winning seventeen of them against larger, faster ships.

The packet service inevitably brought trade to the town. An excellent example of cause and effect is Falmouth's oldest hotel, the Greenbank. It began life as the Ship Inn and, being adjacent to a major pier, took on a similar role for packet passengers as that accorded by coaching inns and, later, railway inns for road and rail travellers. It provided a comprehensive service for its guests, not only getting them to the packets but also providing post chaises for any part of England. Busy and efficient, it earned the complaints of a disgruntled Spanish diplomatic courier in 1808: 'Everybody is in a haste. Either they are going off to the Packets and are hastening their preparation to embark, or they have just arrived and are impatient to be on the way home.' After the packet service came to an end, the inn became a popular place for well-heeled Edwardians. Among them was Kenneth Grahame and it was here that *The Wind in the Willows* was born in the form of letters to his small son, written from the hotel.

One of the attractions of the town are the little alleys, known as 'opes', which run down from Market Street. They, and the slipyards to which they lead, formed the arteries of the town for here were built the wooden sailing ships that created Falmouth's wealth. To the pedestrian, walking slowly along the street and glancing seawards, they present a series of bright, momentary pictures of harbour life.

FROME, SOMERSET

'Beautiful stream' *Anglo-Saxon*
Population: 14,527 *Market:* Wednesday, Saturday

IN 1975 an architectural historian, Colin Amery, published a book unequivocally entitled *The Rape of Britain* in which he showed the effect of 'development' upon thirty British towns. It was an apalling indictment and, in a foreword, John Betjeman asked rhetorically 'What good will this book do? It opens our eyes to what is going on in the midst of us.'

Frome was one of the thirty and both the photographs with which the writer traced the course of destruction, and the text with which he outlined its probable future pattern left the reader convinced that Frome was not so much being raped as murdered. The fact that it has not, the fact that the course of destruction has been halted is, hopefully, an indication that the brutal assault upon English towns during the 1960s and 1970s is coming to an end. In Frome, the author pinpointed two places in particular as being next in line for 'slum clearance': the delightful Badcox Chapel, built in 1825 with its engaging classical façade in Catherine Street, and the seventeenth-century cottages in the area known as Sheppard's Barton. Currently, the chapel is a carpet warehouse, but Sheppard's Barton has been totally rehabilitated – so much so that the danger presented to this and other areas of Frome is gentrification rather than demolition. But so far the town has survived.

The epicentre for the planned destruction was Catherine Hill, the most fascinating part of a fascinating town, high-handedly classed as a 'slum' because most of the buildings are small, old, workers' cottages or modest little shops then in need of renovation. Descending this steep, narrow, winding lane, one half expects to debouch onto a seafront for Frome, like some seaside towns, is built into the side of a hill so sheer that it almost qualifies as a cliff. The lane ends dramatically in the market place: at one moment one is enclosed totally by Catherine Hill, the next there is a vista of a wide, sunlit space lined with dignified buildings, where a small market is held twice weekly.

Running off the market place is a street which combines its medieval name of Cheap (that is, 'market') and medieval purpose, for it is lined on both sides with small shops and cafés in a manner

The Blue House has provided shelter for elderly ladies in Frome for over 250 years. Its name is taken from its previous role as one of the Bluecoat Schools.

that gains the approval of even the modern planner. The attractively varied buildings dating from the fifteenth century onwards are in excellent condition, the lane is wholly traffic free and a tiny sparkling stream, rising in the churchyard above, burbles down its length. The town seems fortunate in being able to use this medieval pattern for modern purposes. The cattle market is tucked away on a great bend of the river outside the town, so one is quite unaware of its presence. When not in use it is occupied by the ubiquitous car park. Even the 'shopping centre' has been integrated into the street scene so that, undistinguished in itself, it does not obtrude but simply does its job.

Frome is essentially a working town with a pattern of industries rising and falling over the centuries. But it was founded by a saint – Aldhelm –

who built the first church here about 685, high above the river. The present church, on the same site though heavily restored in the nineteenth century, can only be described as spectacular, both inside and out. The wealth of sculptured detail is

Shops in Cheap (i.e. 'market') Street. The runnel of water down the centre of the street rises in the churchyard above.

almost Italian in its profusion: particularly outstanding are the great Victorian groups depicting the Via Crucis in the churchyard.

The Domesday Book records that there was already a flourishing market in Frome by the time of the Conquest, and it was wool that brought prosperity to this English town. John Leland visited Frome in the 1530s and remarked that 'There be divers fair stone houses, which standeth mostly by clothying.' Two centuries later, it was even richer through manufacturing clothing, as Daniel Defoe records in the 1720s. The town's wealth had increased 'so

prodigiously in the last 30 years that they have built a new Church and so many new Streets of Houses that Frome is now reckoned to have more people in it than the City of Bath and is very likely to be one of the greatest and wealthiest of Inland Towns in England'.

But the clothiers trade passed to Yorkshire in the early nineteenth century and Frome looked to other sources of income. Bell founding, the gas industry and, above all, printing brought life to the town. Frome is fortunate, too, in its multiplicity of small shops, standing virtually side by side on Catherine Hill. For some reason the giant supermarkets, so destructive alike of the physical town and its trade, never established themselves here.

The remarkable Via Crucis leading up to the church, a product of the Victorian exuberance which transformed the church interior.

GLASTONBURY, SOMERSET

'Woad-growers' fort' *Anglo-Saxon*
Population : 6773 *Market :* Tuesday

THE town plan tells the history of Glastonbury at a glance. An immense open space, approximately square in shape, is lightly fringed with houses on three sides. The houses thicken on the north side to form the High Street, and at the north-west corner appears the characteristically triangular market place.

The square space contains the abbey ruins and the abbot's kitchen, ironically the only structure to remain intact. Despite its purely practical function (even today it could be used as a kitchen so efficient are its vents and funnels) visitors tend to talk in hushed voices in this massive building for it still carries something of its ancient ambience. Elsewhere, all is in ruin: two of the vast pillars of the crossing, where nave, transept and choir meet, tower up from a greensward; the crypt is open to the sky; a few fragments of figured tiles are carefully protected under wooden covers. The foundations have been unearthed, but they are illusory looking smaller than the buildings they supported, and to get a true picture of Glastonbury Abbey it is necessary to inspect the model in the little museum.

For this was a titanic church, bigger than most of

The vast size of Glastonbury Abbey, bigger than most of our surviving cathedrals, is hard to grasp from its ruins. There is, however, an excellent model in the museum.

our cathedrals – longer than St Paul's, taller than Winchester. The tranquillity of the ruins is deceptive for there must have been a great degree of hatred to have brought about so total a destruction. In 1539 Henry VIII decreed, but it was the townsfolk who demolished.

Over the past generation or so, the town has seen more than its fair share of the eccentric, or purely lunatic fringe, for with the decline of formal religion has come the rise of a pseudo-occultry for which Glastonbury was a natural target. People seeking the Holy Grail; people who have found the Holy Grail and want to enshrine it here; people seeking King Arthur's tomb, or the shrine of the Earth Goddess, or a nodal point for UFOs – all have flocked here over the past few decades. In consequence, one would have expected the town to have adopted a kind of candy-floss mysticism, the pyschic equivalent of Disneyland. Yet Glastonbury has remained solidly rooted, a workaday Somerset town whose major industry was, until recently, the preparation of sheep skins.

The superb inn, the George and Pilgrim, stands as a symbol for the whole town. Outside, the inn looks ecclesiastical, and that is reasonable enough for it was built (or, to be exact, rebuilt) by an abbot of Glastonbury some time before 1475 as a hostel for pilgrims. In the manner of these hostels, it was turned into an inn after the Dissolution. Inside, it has adapted, adjusting itself to the changing needs of its clients over the centuries as do all good inns, snugging itself down but yet retaining its character. The stone sill of the windows overlooking the High Street has been chipped and scarred, then polished and blackened by the casual touch of countless human hands over 500 years. The huge internal wall of black oak has scarcely a right-angle to its name. The flagged entrance passage, worn smooth with age, leads via a puzzling angle into the long narrow garden which is a survivor of the burgage plot. The death masks of monks hung high on the wall seem as much memorial as ornament. Nikolaus Pevsner, not a man given to easy compliments, described it as 'one of the most sumptuous of the surviving pre-Reformation inns'. All in all, the George and

The abbot's kitchen. This imposing structure, the only intact survival of the abbey, was so well designed that it could be used for its original purpose today.

24

Pilgrim provides an excellent bridge from the fifth or sixth century to the present day.

The abbey was commenced some time in the late fifth century, the first certain date for the town. As to what happened before, who can say? The adolescence of Christ; the coming of Joseph of Arimathea with his staff, which was later known as the 'Glastonbury thorn'; the burial of King Arthur; the Chalice Well with its miraculous cures; the Celtic goddess with her labyrinth on the Tor – each of these legends disappears, as evanescent as a soap bubble, as it is traced to its source. But together they tell of something very odd that happened here during the opening centuries of medieval England, something probably beyond the skill of archaeologists or historians ever to determine.

From the sixth century onwards we are on fairly safe ground for the monks, with the very practical approach to life of all monastic orders, set about the economic development of the locality. The town declined after their expulsion but revived with the establishment of a tannery in the eighteenth century. The market, established by the abbey gate as was customary, took on a life of its own. The medieval Market Cross was demolished in 1803, an early victim of traffic demands, but was rebuilt in 1846, an excellent example of the potency of this image. It endures even the voracious demands of twentieth-century motorized traffic although the market itself has been, ironically, banished to a car park. The old Market Hall also disappeared, but in 1814 the present elegant Town Hall was built in the market place.

The nineteenth century saw Glastonbury benefiting modestly from the Industrial Revolution. In 1834 a canal linked the town with the Bristol Channel, yielding its place in 1854 to the railway.

The market place. The actual market has been banished to a car park, but the original triangular site is still evident. The cross is a nineteenth-century restoration.

The tanning industry developed into the full-scale manufacture of boots and shoes and, at the same time, a brick and tile industry evolved. Architecturally, this has been a mixed blessing, diluting the ancient grey-stone with modern red brick.

The late twentieth century has been rather less kind to the town. The abbey ruins, mercilessly plundered over the years, are now officially under the care of the Church of England and the town centre is officially an 'Outstanding Conservation Area' in the chilling phrase beloved of bureaucrats. But residential development has somewhat blurred the ancient outlines of the town and, ominously, industry is in retreat. The railway was axed in the 1960s and in the early 1980s the sheepskin industry, for so long a staple trade, began to follow the boot and shoe industry into decline. Yet Glastonbury somehow continues to maintain that wholly intangible ambience that it has preserved for nearly two millenia.

The coat-of-arms over the George and Pilgrim Inn. The façade of the inn, and much of the interior, is a remarkable fifteenth-century survival.

PENZANCE, CORNWALL

'Sacred headland' *Cornish*
Population: 19,521 *Market:* Thursday, Saturday *Cattle:* Tuesday

ECONOMICALLY, it was perhaps Penzance's good fortune to provide a catchy title for a Gilbert and Sullivan opera. Aesthetically, the results have been rather less happy, for it seems that every other building in the town centre has a picture of a pirate sporting an eye patch and carrying a parrot, advertizing the goods for sale within. In sober historic fact, Penzance was indeed plagued by pirates in the sixteenth century. And behind the trashy incitements deemed appropriate for a 'seaside town' lies a solid Cornish town of distinction.

It is an historical paradox that Cornwall, so bare of the signs of ancient urban civilization, should have seen the first contacts with the all-influential culture of the Mediterranean. The Phoenicians

Tucked into Penzance's Mounts Bay is St Michael's Mount, part castle, part church, part private home. Phoenician traders used to bring their wares to this island.

The extraordinary Egyptian House in Chapel Street. Built in the nineteenth-century, it is now the local headquarters of the National Trust.

came here in search of that vital component of bronze – tin – which this gaunt peninsula of Britain produced. Nestling in the 'foot' of that peninsula was a great bay, later called Mounts Bay, which had the singular propensity of virtually emptying itself when the tide went out. The southern traders or their agents brought the precious mineral to the place where Penzance was later to be founded, and then carried it across the dry sands to where deep water began at the island they knew as Ictis, now known as St Michael's Mount (see *Great English Houses* in this series).

Penzance, the furthest west of all English towns, would have begun life as a collection of fishermen's huts sometime in the fourteenth century. Its position on a tranquil bay at the focal point of a number of roads which, though rough, were passable the year round, ensured a modest but certain commercial future. Certainly by the year 1332 there was a weekly market here, together with those fairs which turned a small town into what passed, locally, for a cosmopolitan metropolis.

That tenacious tourist, Celia Fiennes, penetrated as far south as Penzance in the 1690s and left a pleasant portrait of it though, understandably perhaps, getting the origin of its name wrong: 'Pensands is rightly named being all sand about it: it lies

Regency England saw Penzance's development as a watering place and winter resort and it now survives largely through tourism. The terminus of the old Great Western Railway, it is now the helicopter station for the Isles of Scilly.

just as a shore to the main south ocean and being on the side of a hill with a high hill all round the side to the landward, it lookes soe snugg and warme and truely it needs shelter haveing the sea on the other side and little or no fewell.' She noticed with surprise that the people used the local furze for fuel because of the lack of wood.

Northerners have always tended to be somewhat condescending about Cornwall. Daniel Defoe, who visited the town about twenty years after Celia

Though now given over mostly to pleasure craft, the harbour was one of the most important in the West Country. The Spaniards burnt the town down in the sixteenth century.

Fiennes, remarked (and one can almost see his eyebrows rising in sophisticated surprise), 'This town of Pensance is a place of good business, well built and populous, has a good trade and a great many ships belonging to it, notwithstanding it is so remote.' Remote from where, the Cornish might well have asked, for it was an excellent point of departure for Europe and those Channel and Scilly Isles so coveted by both the British and the French. During the last hopeless struggle of the Plantagenet kings to exert their sovreignty over Acquitaine, ships sailed regularly to France from here to back up royal claims. And during the quarrel with Spain, Spanish warships descended on the town and put it to the flames, a fact usually ignored by English chronicler's crowing over the singeing of the King of Spain's beard.

Tardily, the town became a borough by charter in 1614 and was exalted to the status of a stannary town – that is, holding jurisdiction over the tin mines and smelting foundries of west Cornwall – until 1838. It was even allowed to coin money, although this was more in recognition of its relative status in an area remote from the central authority than of its true importance. But the wealth that was pouring into England in the north passed Penzance by: even the turnpike roads came no further south than Falmouth. As with so many other towns, the railway brought life. And still does. The grey granite station, tucked between town and beach, is one of the few surviving in Cornwall and it has been given a new lease of life by the fact that a modern helicopter port, serving the Isles of Scilly, has been established in the town.

An open, blowy, breezy town is the impression one takes away. The Brontës' mother, who lived in one of the elegant Georgian houses, must have looked back upon its clean, windswept freshness with deep nostalgia from the plague spot in Yorkshire which eventually killed her. There is nothing dramatic here to compare with its somewhat theatrical counterpart, St Ives, on the north coast (though the extraordinary Egyptian House which accommodates the National Trust locally must lay claim to an outstanding example of eccentricity). Penzance is, in short, a town that has managed to maintain its character even in its current role of 'seaside town'.

SHEPTON MALLET, SOMERSET

'Malet's sheep farm' *Anglo-Saxon*
Population: 6306 Market: Friday

IT is one of the mysteries of urban life that when two equal towns of similar size are subjected to similar pressures, one will somehow retain its identity and dignity while the other will undergo a deleterious change of greater or lesser degree. Compared to its neighbours Wells, Glastonbury and Frome, Shepton Mallet has a faintly woe-begone, slightly down-at-heel air. Like Glastonbury and Frome, it too suffered a decline in the wool industry after the eighteenth century, but where the others buckled down and found alternative employment, Shepton Mallet never quite caught up with itself. Down by the tiny River Sheppey (a remarkably small energy source for the affluence it once brought the town) the dilapidation resembles that of one of the poorer Italian hill towns – not unattractive, certainly, but curiously out of keeping with the other trim towns of Somerset. Even the great railway viaduct that crosses the valley and provides a dramatic backdrop to the town, now that its function has gone with the closing of the line, is a reminder of the distant past.

Yet there is some good modern architecture in the town centre, and some sensitive town planning. The Centre, the complex given to the town by the Showering family, would be outstanding in a place many times the size of Shepton Mallet. It is, in effect, a twentieth-century Assembly Room, a boldly modern building boldly placed in the very heart of the town. Occupying the sensitive site between the ancient churchyard and the market place, it could have been disastrous. Instead, it adds

Shepton Mallet viaduct. The axeing of railway lines has reduced the viaduct to the status of a museum exhibit, but it makes a superb backcloth to the town.

Skilful pedestrianization has restored the old Market Square to its function as a meeting place. The cross was built in 1500 and is still used by traders.

a strong, contemporary ingredient to an already rich townscape.

The recent pedestrianization of the market place has the attraction of pure logic, for this tiny forum now looks as though it has always been here, just where it was needed. Freed of its blight of traffic, its subtle harmonies become evident for buildings that cover at least five centuries somehow combine into a unit. The hexagonal Market Cross, built in 1500, is modest compared to that of Chichester or Salisbury but it was designed on the same lines, protecting traders from the elements now as efficiently as in the past. At one time even wives were put up for sale here as well as the more prosaic market goods. Nearby is a most unusual survival, the covered bench or table known as a Shamble, the forerunner of today's flimsy stall (one wonders why such an eminently practical and attractive design fell out of use here and elsewhere). The mountback or quack-stage, a platform whence preachers discoursed, has gone from the front of the Bell Inn but small shops, the public library and a couple of inns all surround the square, keeping it a point of human contact.

The lands that were to form the town were granted to the abbey of Glastonbury before the Norman Conquest, but it was not until 1234 that it obtained its first market charter from the king. The 'Mallet' of the town's name refers to the name of a Norman family, related to the Conqueror himself. A Baron Mallet was one of the five powerful men who forced King John to sign the Magna Carta, earning that shifty monarch's undying enmity. Traditionally, the town always seems to have followed a sturdily independent policy, sometimes to its considerable cost. A parliamentary town in a strongly royalist area, one of the first battles of the Civil War was fought in the market place, the embattled merchants, shop keepers and artisans of the town eventually chasing the royalists back to their stronghold in Wells. Some forty years later, during the so-called Pitchfork Rebellion of 1685, the market place saw more bloodshed. The town had welcomed the Duke of Monmouth on his ill-fated and ill-planned march to Sedgemoor, and paid for his defeat: a dozen local men were hanged on gibbets erected in the market place, then quartered and their remains boiled in salt, 'half a bushel to each traitor, tarr to tarr them with', in order to preserve them for the edification of their fellow citizens.

Wool brought capital, shaping the town. The tiny, but fast-moving river drove the small mills; weavers' cottages climbed the steep hill with the larger houses of mill-owners still part of the townscape. The inevitable decline in the nineteenth century brought violence, with unemployed workers rioting in the streets and setting fire to the mills. They were powerless to restore that particular means of livelihood and the town gradually returned to the oldest of all industries, that of agricultural production with cheese-making and cider-brewing pre-eminent – not enough to bring great wealth, but sufficient to cushion the impact of change.

But architectural evidence of the period of prosperity is easily found: the large seventeenth-century building known as Longbridge House down by the river; the gabled terrace called Great Ostry; the grammar school, built in 1627 and now the vicarage, and its near companions, the solidly comfortable almshouses. Drawing the whole together is the church, sombre without, light and gracious within, its fabric bearing all the marks of its long history from Saxon times to the twentieth century, including the destruction wrought by the parliamentary iconoclasts of the seventeenth century – the debit column of the town's independence.

TOTNES, DEVON

'Totta's headland' *Anglo-Saxon*
Population: 5627 *Market:* Tuesday *Cattle:* Friday

THE name, the topography and the imposing castle of this small town spell out its origins. The site is indeed a headland with the Dart coiling round it, a natural site for a stronghold. Founded as a royal burh in the reign of Edgar (959–975), the line of the existing town walls follows the old Saxon earthworks. The castle itself is the product of the invaders, the Normans, placed here both to overawe the townsmen and act as a garrison on this vital section of river. It is, unusually, a shell keep on its green mound, unusually, for these early, relatively hasty forms of fortification were often later developed into the full square keep. In Totnes, the shell remains today much as it would have appeared in the early fourteenth century when the original thirteenth-century edifice was reconstructed. Throughout the long centuries of its life it remained in private hands until 1947 when it was transferred to the then Ministry of Works.

Saxon burhs either withered away, after their military function ended, or developed into towns depending purely upon their location. The new town's position on the Dart ensured its success and, until well into the sixteenth century, it flourished as a port until the silting of the river limited its use. Three centuries later it again received an economic blow with the coming of the railway in 1847. In most towns, this phenomenon stimulated trade: here, the railway simply stole what river trade remained without bringing anything in its place. In consequence, the town declined, the population sinking by nearly a quarter to a little over 3000. But what was a financial tragedy proved an aesthetic blessing for the town entered the late twentieth century, and the era of protection by conservation, relatively unchanged.

Totnes falls into two main sections, the result of unusually early suburban expansion. As early as the thirteenth century houses began to appear outside the East Gate, continuing the line of the High Street

Totnes, tucked between the brooding hill, which once protected and dominated the town, and the winding river which once brought it wealth.

Totnes Castle is an excellent (and rare) example of a surviving Norman shell keep
on its mound or motte.

Despite its Regency appearance, the East Gate
that crosses Fore Street is part of
the original fortifications.

and, in due course, becoming known as Fore Street. Happily, the East Gate still survives. In most towns, the late eighteenth and early nineteenth century saw wholesale destruction of town gates to facilitate traffic movement: with unusual restraint, Totnes retained the upper half of the gate while widening the lower half into an attractive Tudor-style arch. The façade was then covered in the fashionable stucco, but the beautiful room behind, with its sixteenth-century linenfold panelling and carved portraits of Henry VIII and Anne Boleyn, still remains.

In the 1830s a further development across the river gave the town a third section. A new bridge was begun in 1826 (its architect, Charles Fowler, later designed London's Covent Garden market), and 'Bridgetown' was the name given to the new settlement that it created on the other side of the river. It received a considerable social fillip when the Duke of Somerset built a great inn there, the Seymour Arms, as a rival to the seventeenth-century Seven Stars inn in Fore Street.

The building of the parish church was particularly well documented, and what emerges from the records is that the church was very much the expression of the will of the townsfolk. They even laboured in the quarries and provided transport at their own expense. A building intended to express civic pride had to outshine its neighbours and the master mason, Roger Growdon, was specifically instructed to inspect the towers of neighbouring churches and produce one even better. He did so, copying but improving. Within the church, they went one better. The rood screen would be impressive even in wood, but the people of Totnes decreed that it should be made in stone. The rood loft was equally impressive: this actually survived the iconoclasts of the seventeenth century, but fared less well with the Victorian 'restorers' in 1865.

Curiously, for a town so strongly aware of its corporate identity, Totnes has a relatively unimpressive Guildhall. The present hall, built in 1553, took the place of what was evidently a cramped and meagre structure but even this sixteenth-century edifice is tucked away, relying for much of its exterior dignity upon pillars brought from elsewhere. The whole is undoubtedly picturesque but, in terms of civic grandeur, not to be compared with that other port, King's Lynn, or many a contemporary inland town.

Totnes evolved for its market the delightful, and thoroughly practical covered rows which are locally called 'piazzas' (an evident confusion with the colonnaded walks that surround Italian piazzas and provided a model). The only other English town to develop this eminently sensible device for the uncertain English climate is Chester. The Butterwalk, on the north side of the High Street, shows an unbroken line of these pillars, each group related to the house it supports and therefore of a different design to its fellows, but the whole combining into a visual unity.

This ancient place at the head of the Dart estuary still maintains its tradition as a busy market town and shopping centre for the South Hams.

The sixteenth-century Guildhall is tucked away in this delightful courtyard. The stone pillars were imported later to give added dignity to a modest structure.

WELLS, SOMERSET

'Springs' Anglo-Saxon
Population : 8374 Market : Saturday

SET in the pavement of Wells' market place, not far from the Penniless Porch of the cathedral, is a line of brass Olympic symbols stretching for exactly 22 feet $2\frac{1}{4}$ inches. Beside it a plaque records: 'This represents the world record ladies' long jump made by Mary Bignal Rand, a native of this city, to win the Gold Medal of the Olympic Games, Tokyo 1964.' The donor identifies himself or herself simply by the initials 'T.W.W'.

The memorial tells the visitor two things about this exquisite little city: an intense pride of citizenship finding expression in a living centre. Towering over the market place is one of Europe's great cathedrals, so crammed with treasures as to create a

Situated outside the main entrance to the great cathedral and in the very heart of the town, Wells' market place still provides a lively social and economic function.

sense of frustration to all but the most dedicated visitor, one prepared to spend days rather than hours exploring it. Adjoining it is the bishop's palace, moated, ancient, almost impossibly picturesque with its trained swans. But it is to the market place that one instinctively gravitates, using it as a point of departure to explore this working miniature of an ideal city, but returning to it again and again.

It is unusually well planned and well balanced for an English market place. Three roads lead into it but only one, the High Street, carries much traffic so that it is, for all practical purposes, a tranquil cul-de-sac, closed by the massive cathedral gate on one side, flanked on another by a range of great inns and the Town Hall, and on the third side by attractive houses dating from the fifteenth century onwards. The central feature is, again, rather unusual in an English town – a large working fountain. Its present shape is that of an eighteenth-century grotto, for it was built in 1799, but it draws on the cold, clear, sweet water of the springs that give the city its name, and which feed the sparkling stream that runs down the High Street.

The town has a royal foundation. Ina, king of the West Saxons, built a church beside the springs which rose at the foot of the Mendips halfway between Cheddar, where he had his palace, and Glastonbury, where he was rebuilding the colossal abbey. The town became the seat of a bishop in 909 but the Normans moved the bishopric to Bath and for over two centuries thereafter, until the mid 1230s, it migrated between the two cities. Bishop Jocelin of Wells, however, firmly settled himself in the city and, with the real intention of remaining there began work on the palace. A compromise was eventually reached, with the bishop taking the title of both Bath and Wells, but living in Wells: the palace is therefore probably the oldest inhabited building in the country. The cathedral itself was begun in 1180, the first truly 'English' cathedral to be erected. The addition of the great central tower in 1315 nearly brought disaster for the foundations were never intended to take so great a weight and the tower began to settle. But out of this arose one of the cathedral's most distinctive and beautiful features,

The cathedral from Tor Hill. For years there was rivalry between Bath and Wells as to which should be the capital of the Diocese, resolved only when the bishop took the title of both Bath and Wells.

the swooping, soaring, inverted arches under the crossing, inserted as supports.

The riches of the cathedral seem all but inexhaustible from the extraordinary carved portrait gallery of the west front to the great clock with its charging knights, its astronomical dial, and the lugubrious Jack Blandiver sounding the quarters with his hands and feet. Outside, the palace is a world in itself, still operating as the heart of a great diocese. Matching it on a smaller scale is Vicar's Close. This was once the College of Vicars' Choral, forming an enclave of its own. Many of the forty-two cells have been turned into ordinary dwelling houses but one, No 22, was restored by a local antiquary as a model of the original cell unit.

But, despite the relative size of the cathedral and its establishment in so small a city, Wells has been able to maintain a vigorous independent civic life, centred round its 'own' church. The Parish Church of St Cuthbert was the home of the trade guilds and adjoining the churchyard is a building that is part almshouse, part guildhall. The clearcut distinction between town and cathedral is responsible for the palace moat, a unique defence for a building actually in a town. In the fourteenth century strong differ-

ences of opinion between townsfolk and clergy led the bishop, Ralph of Shrewsbury, to fortify his palace. Ironically, the fortifications were never used during the turbulent Middle Ages, but proved distinctly valuable when the Reform Act rioters destroyed the bishop's palace in Bristol in 1831. The Bishop of Bath and Wells gratefully raised his fourteenth-century drawbridge.

Vicar's Close. Once the College of Vicars' Choral and dating back to the fourteenth century, this is reputed to be the oldest inhabited residential street in England.

THE SOUTH AND SOUTH-EAST

FARNHAM, SURREY

'Fern estate' *Anglo-Saxon*
Population: 35,289 Market: First Saturday in the month

ALTHOUGH all towns are, of necessity, made from a variety of materials, with innumerable variations of colour and texture within the materials themselves, some towns fix themselves in the mind as being of one substance. One thinks of Stamford as a stone town, of Stratford in terms of timber, Ludlow in terms of stucco. The dominant material in Farnham that binds all else together is brick, much of it now 300 years old, its mellow shades ranging from yellow to old rose.

Farnham is one of England's few planned towns for it was laid out by the Bishop of Winchester in the twelfth century. Its grid pattern resembles that of a Roman castrum, a quite accidental result which nevertheless gives a true, urban feeling to what is in fact a very small town. The traditional markets today have dwindled in importance, with new emphasis on those so-called craft markets which

Farnham town centre. The Town Hall was refurbished in 1905, though now without municipal function. Castle Street, the old market street, lies to the left.

have risen in the past decade or so as a reaction to the increasing mechanization of society. But Farnham's brick-built beauty owes everything to the fact that it was once the largest corn market in England. Daniel Defoe, who rode round England in the 1720s compiling his own personal Domesday book, recorded that on one occasion he counted 1100 teams of horses hauling corn wagons to the market – a total, he reckoned, of 44,000 bushells of wheat. The market declined in the 1750s when it became cheaper to send corn to London by sea, but for about half a century money poured into the town, allowing it to transform itself from a medieval into a Georgian town. And even after the corn market declined, the hops for which the district was famous brought in more income, and left a distinctive architectural feature in the form of the high, narrow entrances to yards through which the laden hop wagons were brought. The autumn picking, when the town was crowded with itinerant 'hoppers', together with the weekly cattle market and the thrice-annual fairs brought life and increased commercial wealth to the town until the end of the nineteenth century. A decline set in with the rise of Kentish hops but this in turn was arrested by the arrival of the railway and the evolution of a new human species, the commuter.

The vast keep of the bishop's castle was totally destroyed after the Civil War, but his beautiful palace survived. Farnham has many attractive streets, but Castle Street is undoubtedly its gem. Its proportions, created for the pragmatic needs of a market place, are superb. The broad, handsome thoroughfare dwindles fairly rapidly as it passes the castle, disappearing between great trees, imparting a sense of mystery to a humdrum market street. The

Although the outskirts of the town have become blurred, this aerial view shows the grid plan created by the Bishop of Winchester in the twelfth century.

grid pattern of the roads, instead of producing monotony, seems to provide a series of stages for the endless acts of the urban drama.

Farnham is famous as the birthplace of that rumbustious polemicist, William Cobbett, buried in the church a few hundred yards from the house (now the Jolly Farmer inn) where he was born. But splendid writer though Cobbett was, the lesser-known George Sturt gives a better, indeed an unrivalled picture of life in a small town before the development of modern transport. Sturt was born in Farnham in 1863 and died there in 1927. His friend Arnold Bennet described him as 'a wheelwright by trade and an author by profession' and certainly Sturt gave up wheelwrighting with what seems a sigh of relief in 1920, saying 'authorship seemed easier than genuine work'. Ironically, perhaps, his book *The Wheelwright's Shop* proved the most successful of all and has never been out of print since it appeared in 1923.

Throughout his life Sturt maintained intimate, yet thoroughly unsentimental links with this small market town and its rural hinterland. And no writer conveyed as he did, in his immense *Journal*, the feeling of claustrophobia that is the reverse of the intimacy provided by a small town. It is precisely this element of criticism that makes Sturt so valuable a chronicler of country town life during a period of immense social change. He was no starry-eyed romanticist escaping from a big city and intent upon portraying a rural paradise but, instead, a man who knew the sheer *ennui* of small-town life, who experienced the gossiping malice born of too close, too prolonged human contact and yet was able to treat it all objectively, weaving it into his narratives to make a general, permanent statement about the human condition. His wheelwright's shop is still in Farnham, but used now as a motorcycle repair shop, an odd illustration of the toughness of human continuity.

HYTHE, KENT

'Landing place' *Anglo-Saxon*
Population : 12,210 *Market :* Monday, Friday, Saturday

THE town's Anglo-Saxon name provides an immediate pointer to its origins. Viewed geologically the whole of this section of coastline is undergoing endless change as wind, tide and rivers together work to sculpt the flat marshlands. Any firm landfall in the maze of mud-flats, shingle banks and ridges in the Stour estuary would have inevitably developed as the site of a community. The original 'landing

The architectural variety of English towns : pottery tiles, 'Essex' weather-boarding and flint.

place' here – the one which Julius Caesar would have known – was further inland at what is now West Hythe. But gradually the estuary silted up and, as it did so, the 'landing place' or 'hythe' moved to its present location.

And if the town's name explains its location, the ship on its borough coat-of-arms refers to its membership of that proud and ancient community, the Cinque Ports. It is one of the engaging quirks of

English history that we should use a French name for an organization very largely intended to defend us from the French. It was the Norman kings who grouped together five towns along the south-east coast, giving them considerable municipal privileges in return for the obligation of providing ships and men. Their primary task was to defend this vulnerable stretch of coast, but they were also

The gradual silting up of the estuary resulted in Hythe

expected to provide transport for the English king's attempts to add France to the English crown.

Hythe has the oldest charter of the Cinque Ports, dated 1278, but in common with most such charters it is simply a surviving record of privileges and obligations conferred much earlier. But the very reasons that had brought this embryonic port into being, some time before the ninth century, had brought it to an end by 1450 when silting totally destroyed the harbour. Today, the old town is a good half mile inland and a complete new township, laid out with mathematical precision, now lies between old Hythe and the sea.

Medieval military obligations might have given Hythe its distinctive civic status, but it was the threat of Napoleonic invasion that created much of its modern topography. The most obvious example is the Royal Military Canal and, looking at this waterway on the map, it becomes immediately evident that it is not a 'canal' as is generally understood by the term: it winds and curves in a manner no canal ever does without the strongest geographical reasons. The purpose of the curves are in fact military, allowing enfilading fire to be brought to bear on troops attempting to cross.

The canal is, in effect, a moat, stretching from Hythe to Rye, and protected with a first line of defence in the form of the massive Martello Towers

moving further eastward to the present shoreline. This view shows one of the towers of the Napoleonic defences.

that are a feature of this entire coastline. In the event of invasion the marshland could be flooded, the whole town becoming a military base. We have a vivid description of it from the pen of William Cobbett in 1823. The architect of the scheme was the prime minister, William Pitt, and Cobbett loathed everything that Pitt and his administration stood for. He described, with mocking incredulity, the canal: 'Here is a canal, made for the length of thirty miles, to *keep out the French*: those armies which had so often crossed the Rhine and the Danube were to be kept back by a canal thirty feet wide at most!' He jeered at the Martello Towers, 'ridiculous things which I dare say cost five, perhaps ten thousand pounds each ... Hythe is half barracks: the hills are covered with barracks. All along the coast there are works of some sort of another: walls of immense dimensions, masses of stone brought and put into piles.'

Today those anti-invasion structures have acquired a patina of antique charm. The threat of war also created one of the town's most beautiful natural features, the magnificent avenues of Huntingdon elms. The War Office planted these in 1820 to provide stocks for the old muzzle-loading rifles.

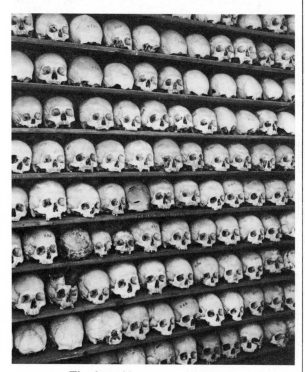

The charnel house – part of the large collection of skulls in the crypt of St Leonard's Church.

On the map, the town seems to be little more than an extension of Folkestone, but its heart is in good shape, a distinctive Kentish town huddled comfortably at the feet of its parish church. There are still traces of Norman work in the church, but its most outstanding feature – outstanding, indeed, in any English church – is the remarkable thirteenth-century chancel, soaring high above the nave. And in keeping with the town's truculent maritime tradition is the enormous iron chest in the church, reputedly salvaged from an Armada galleon. It must have been intended to hold some impressive treasure for there are no less than eleven bolts operated by the central lock, bolts which still fly back with a tremendous crash when the weighty key is turned.

And, testimony to the English love of eccentricity, Hythe is the northern terminus of 'the world's smallest railway'. The Romney, Hythe and Dymchurch Railway was built in 1925 by a racing

It is necessary to compare the size of a child with that of the engine to realise that this is in fact a model railway – the famous Romney, Hythe and Dymchurch line.

motorist, Captain J.E.P.Howey. Some $13\frac{1}{2}$ miles of track were laid on the conveniently flat marshland at a cost of £2000 a mile – relatively cheap for the only engineering work required was the bridging of dykes. Twelve locomotives operate the line, each of them 5 feet in height and a scale model of one of the famous locomotives of their day.

LEWES, EAST SUSSEX

'Hills' Anglo-Saxon
Population: 13,770 *Market:* Monday, including cattle

WELL within living memory, Lewes used to be the scene of one of the most hair-raising of Bonfire Night celebrations. At that time they coincided with the municipal elections and bore far more resemblance to organized riots than they do to the innocuous Guy Fawkes' Night activities held today. The violence took place in towns all over England, but Lewes was outstanding among them. After the Bonfire Night celebration of 1847, 100 Metropolitan police were called in, the Riot Act read and the hospitals filled with injured. In 1910, an octogenarian remembers, the highlight of the occasion was the rolling of a barrel of blazing tar down the steep High Street. The violence has departed from

The castle still dominates the town. The unusual double motte structure, with one mound overlooking the town and the other the river, is illustrated clearly in this aerial view.

Bonfire Night is still a major event in the town. The 'pioneer group' leading the procession here traditionally make their own costumes.

the occasion, but the presence of six active Bonfire Night societies, each planning processions with fancy dress, tableaux, bands and fireworks shows how deeply the custom is rooted in the town's history.

This compact, hill-top town, still given shape by its city walls and crowned by an immense castle, is urban to the core despite its relatively small size. Too many English towns of similar size have become watered down in character, neither village nor town in feeling. Lewes, one suspects, would still be a 'town' if the population were reduced to the hundreds.

Saxon in origin, Lewes was one of King Alfred's fortress towns, established about 890 as a defence against the Danes. Most of these so-called 'Burghal Hidage' towns disappeared, or reverted to village status after the military need had gone but some, like Lewes, took root and flourished. Just before the Norman Conquest there were 127 burgesses (a multiplication of perhaps five would give the population of the town) and the importance of this small, fortified place just 9 miles from the coast is demonstrated by the fact that the Conqueror gave it to one of his closest associates, William de Warenne. He was probably the king's own son-in-law and it was he who began work on the castle.

The vast building was dismantled in 1620, its materials sold to the citizens to build their own houses so that there is an homogeneity of building stone throughout the town. But still sufficient survives of the original structure to give some idea of its scale, and it is possible to trace such details as the portcullis grooves even though the drawbridge has long since gone. It is, unusually, a double motte construction with one motte or mound overlooking the River Ouse and the other commanding the entrance to the town. It is well worthwhile climbing to the keep for from here one can obtain a bird's eye view of the town's strategic position and, in particular, that vital place in English history where the Battle of Lewes was fought in 1264. Here, below Mount Harry, the forces of Simon de Montfort defeated those of Henry III, laying the foundation of parliamentary government.

The little town is so rich in architectural history that the Council for British Archaeology listed it among those fifty-one English towns whose preservation is a matter of national importance and urgency. It is mostly eighteenth-century, but with some outstanding earlier buildings. Descending from the castle, the first major building encountered is Shelley's Hotel. This began life in 1577 as the Vine Inn (there are still contemporary murals inside illustrating a vine, and the original wooden sign is preserved in the museum), but was substantially altered internally in the eighteenth century when it became the home of the Shelley family. Further on is the town's showpiece, Keere Street, a narrow cobbled lane – the very epitome of the English town street – descending steeply to Southover Grange. This is one of the many English private houses built from the great plunder of the monasteries. The Caen stone of which it is built was taken from Lewes Priory by William Newton in 1572. He was an ancestor of Isaac Newton and, in its time, the house also sheltered John Evelyn, the diarist, whose grandmother married a Newton.

Just beyond the railway line are the remains of the priory, apart from the castle the major medieval relic of the town. This too was built by William de Warenne and his wife Gundrada. Once extremely affluent and prestigious, it was important enough to act as headquarters for Henry III. After the battle, de Montfort's men vandalized the priory, but it survived and prospered until Henry VIII's hatchet man, Thomas Cromwell, got to work on it. In most cases, the physical destruction of the monasteries was left to the locals – one could always depend on masons finding a use for expensive quarried stone. But Cromwell seemed to have had a special hatred for Lewes Priory, even bringing in an Italian engineer to demolish the place. So totally was it destroyed that its very site was forgotten until 1845 when excavations for the Lewes–Bright railway uncovered the foundations. The navvies also discovered bones, subsequently identified as those of de Warenne and Gundrada, and these were given decent burial in Southover Church. In recent years the priory has been the subject of archaeological excavation and restoration: the Great Gate is of particular interest, being built of Sussex marble.

Lewes is no fossilized antiquity but an important rural metropolis, somehow combining an impressive number of administrative functions (it is the County Town of East Sussex) with an ability to pursue its own life. Indeed, it nearly fell victim to its own prosperity when the crush of traffic threatened to throttle the life out of its markets. The creation of a bypass, however, eased the pressure, and the sound of cattle, and of humans bargaining, continue to give life to the town centre. An example of

Southover Grange, a product of the plunder of the monasteries. Its Caen stone was taken from the priory by William Newton (an ancestor of Isaac Newton) in 1572.

Lewes's skill in combining a number of roles is the Town Hall. It was built in 1893 and, at first sight, seems a typically brash, Victorian building. But inside is a superb Elizabethan staircase, and deep below are the fourteenth-century cellars which were used as a prison for the Protestant martyrs, burned to death by Bloody Mary. Their memorial is visible high on Cliffe Hill, and the probability is that those rumbustious bonfire celebrations are as much in the memory of these Christian martyrs as of the incompetent arsonist, Guy Fawkes.

NEWPORT, ISLE OF WIGHT

'New town' Anglo-Saxon
Population : 23,570 Market : Tuesday

IN his 'biography' of the Isle of Wight Paul Hyland quotes a piece of dialect first recorded about the 1860s: 'Why, I can mind the time we onny used to goo to Nippert twice or free times a year, wi' a carriage o' corn and it used to take us all day to git there and back. We used to think ver [very] near zo much on't as people do now to goo to 'Meriky.' Today, the speaker's great-grandson quite likely does go almost casually to 'Meriky, but he will still regard Newport as the capital of a little island kingdom.

The Isle of Wight is barely a stone's throw from the mainland. The Solent is not as wide as the Severn at Bristol but, in crossing it, a sea-change takes place and suddenly one is 'abroad'. Until recently the Isle was classed with Hampshire for administrative purposes: its railway system is served by London's superannuated tube trains; the difference between Wight and Hampshire dialects is evident only to the speakers. But the Isle of Wight is, quite noticeably, socially separate from the mainland and that feeling of 'foreignness', so attractive to visitors, is a delightful characteristic of Newport.

The history of the island is as long as the history of the mainland. Indeed, one of Newport's showpieces is a Roman villa incongruously tucked away in a suburban street. But Newport is a relative newcomer for, until the twelfth century, the island was governed from the vast castle of Carisbrooke. Some kind of community would probably have straggled into being at the confluence of the Medina river and Lukely brook a mile or so from the castle, but it was not until 1177 that Richard de Redvers, as lord of the manor, gave a charter to 'novus burgus meus de Medina'. By the irony of history the village of Carisbrooke is now virtually a suburb of the novus burgus, the 'new port' which de Redvers intended to serve his castle.

The Medina river was the town's lifeline, the means by which sizeable ships could come right into the heart of this diamond-shaped island. Newport is almost exactly at the centre, a situation which has saved it from the fate of the towns along the east coast. There, the combined road and rail links have created a wearisomely familiar subtopia with an almost endless sequence of buildings from Ryde in the north to Ventnor in the south. Sun, sea and sand worshippers tend to remain along that coast so that, although the island is all but overwhelmed by tourists in the season, Newport maintains its identity. People go there because they want to go there, not simply because it provides a platform for other activities.

Carisbrooke is medieval, flanked by the castle and priory church towering above the village. Newport,

The main body of the Town Hall is an elegant Regency building by John Nash. The incongruous tower was added to commemorate Queen Victoria's Jubilee.

despite an abundance of older buildings, notably inns, seems to be largely nineteenth century, specifically Victorian in atmosphere. Understandably so, for Queen Victoria conferred respectability upon the island and settled at Osborne just down the river. It was at her direct request that a rather sentimental statue to the tragic little Princess Elizabeth was put up in the newly rebuilt parish church in 1856. The princess had been imprisoned with her father, Charles I, at Carisbrooke Castle, surviving his execution by less than two years before dying at the age of fifteen in September 1650. 'As to the boy, it would be better to bind him to a trade', said Cromwell laconically when he heard the news. Princess Elizabeth's grave was totally forgotten until discovered by accident in 1793. During the rebuilding of the church, it was said that her coffin was housed at one stage in the near-by Wheatsheaf Inn. A curious coincidence, if true, for just opposite the Wheatsheaf is the Rose and Crown where, according to legend, a brave follower of Charles I gave him a rose as he was being taken to Carisbrooke.

For a staunchly parliamentary town, Newport has many royal associations. St James's Square has a splendidly flamboyant piece of Victoriana erected in the queen's honour. Another, more misguided outburst of patriotism saddled John Nash's elegant Regency Guildhall with a massive clocktower put up for the Jubilee and the new and excellent public library bears the name of Lord Louis Mountbatten, late governor of the Isle.

Newport is still, one feels, a working town even though the cattle market was moved out of the centre in 1927. It is still possible to follow the medieval street pattern: one could, indeed, use Speed's plan of 1611 to find one's way around the twentieth-century town centre. Newport is facing the problem that confronts most of our smaller ports and harbours: what does one do with port facilities that are no longer required? Tourism has undoubtedly contributed here. The little quay has been attractively laid out: some of the defunct warehouses have been turned into an arts centre and work has begun on the reclamation of the banks of the Medina. But craft still use the basin and though most are now pleasure boats, their handling requires the same expertise as working craft, their presence keeping the little port alive. And under that confident Victorian monument the market goes its way, bringing the little square to life on a Tuesday, trading the produce of this rich island.

Socially, Queen Victoria put the Isle of Wight on the map. This massive, exuberant memorial marks the islanders' gratitude to their queen.

Carisbrooke Castle. Newport came into existence to supply the castle but gradually took on independent life. Charles I spent the last year of his life in captivity here.

RYE, EAST SUSSEX

'Island' Anglo-Saxon
Population: 4293 *Market:* Thursday *Cattle:* Wednesday

THE best approach to Rye is by train along one of the intimate little local tracks that once bound all England together. Leaving Ashford, the train swings across a great green plain that, oddly, gives the sensation of being at sea. And that was exactly what the plain was less than three centuries ago. Rye looms up, looking like a headland and, again, this was its original form in the geologically recent past. The sea retreated all along this coastline stranding Rye and its neighbour Winchelsea, and approaching

The town's showpiece, Mermaid Street, took its name from the superb Mermaid Inn on the right. Nineteenth-century photographs taken from the same standpoint show the harbour at the bottom.

The clock tower of Rye's parish church. The Quarter Boys, who strike the bells on the quarter hour, were added in 1775. The clock itself dates from 1562.

precipitous rock upon which the town was built remains to give it a permanent shape. The town slopes from east (seaward) to west (landward). There is a small harbour on the River Rother at its feet and the railway station, too, is tucked away on this western side. On leaving the station, one starts climbing.

The little town's proud official name is 'Rye Royal' for it was a royal manor in 1247 and became a royal borough in 1289. This was when it received its charter, granting it among other things the lucrative market rights – Wednesday for general markets and Thursday for cattle (nowadays reversed). The charter also gave it a most unusual distinction: as a royal manor its bailiff had been entitled to carry a mace and, as a borough, its mayor also received that right. The mayor was, ex officio, the king's bailiff and instead of extinguishing one right, the town combined the two. In consequence Rye, smaller than many a village, is entitled to two maces in the mayoral processions.

The visitor to a town so rich in historical architecture can be disorientated even in so small a place as Rye. The town has therefore adopted that idea of a 'heritage centre' which up to now has been adopted only by major cities. This houses an exquisite, large-scale model of the town, illustrated as a *son et lumière*, over which the spectator hovers god-like as a brilliant commentary unfolds its history and now one, now another part of the model comes to life.

Rye can be explored comfortably in a day, and provides enough material to warrant a lifetime's study. The town was part of the armoured front that the English presented to their enemies across the Channel; the French burnt it down completely in 1377, stone buildings alone surviving that particular raid. The monumental walls and towers remain to give some idea of what this fortress town once looked like.

But it was a trading town, too. On the recreation ground known as The Salts the citizens used to bank the fields and let in the sea, thus producing valuable salt by evaporation. And the local fishmongers not only kept firm control of the local market but were even able to prevent the fishmongers of London from buying Rye fish to sell retail. The inns of Rye are famous, nourished by the fact that the town was a stage post. Outstanding even among them is the Mermaid, which has somehow survived the twin evils of 'modernization' and fake antiquity, its woodwork harmonious and mellow with age. It is an

these towns across that wide green plain is like crossing the dead sea bottoms of Edgar Rice Burroughs's Martian novels.

But though the sea has long since gone, the

The massive defences of Rye are still visible above the little river harbour. The sea, which created the town, is now ten minutes away due to the changing coastline.

inn in the great tradition and not simply a place for the ingestion of alcoholic beverages.

The town is a lodestone for tourists, but has not been swamped by them: Sussex voices still dominate in pub and market place. The outstanding historic buildings are conserved, rather than preserved – that is, they still have a function and are not fossilized at some arbitrary point in time. An excellent example of this is Lamb House. The Lamb family, mayors of the town for over a century, occupied this house from 1723 to 1832. The street front is plain, almost austere though dignified, but behind that passive wall is a superb English garden. Henry James wrote his writhingly complex novels in a garden house there; another novelist, Rumer Godden, later restored the house, now owned by the National Trust yet still used as a living home. In the same way, Rye is a living town pursuing its own business, though well aware of its attraction for visitors, its seafaring and smuggling past apparent in every twisting cobbled street of this ancient little market town.

West Street, Rye. The house closing the vista is Lamb House, where the writer Henry James made his home.

SHAFTESBURY, DORSET

'Sceaft's fort' *Anglo-Saxon*
Population : 4942 *Market :* Thursday

As with so many place-names, there is some doubt as to the original meaning of 'Shaftesbury' for it can mean either 'fort established by a man called Sceaft' or 'fort built on the point of a promontory'. There is, however, no doubt as to why somebody built a fort just here. The road from Salisbury, 20 miles away, climbs slowly to the west – and then just stops for it comes to the edge of a tremendous sandstone cliff. When, towards the end of the ninth century, King Alfred was seeking a site for another of the forts in the chain he was building, this sandstone cliff presented itself as a natural site.

In most other places time, subtly working on the landscape, and an expanding population, obscure the reason for the siting of a town. Not so with Shaftesbury. Standing on the point of the promontory one can see, lying at the foot of the cliff and stretching mistily into the blue distance, that same country that Alfred was seeking to defend from the invading Danes. Just behind the observer is the immense abbey which Alfred founded and in which he installed his daughter, Aethelgiva, as its first abbess. Once, this tiny town in its rich countryside was the very heart of England, but today few are aware of its historic past and the treasures in its abbey. Aelgiva, Edmund Ironside's wife, is buried here; so was Edward the Martyr, murdered at Corfe Castle (his bones are now, ironically, in the possession of the Midland Bank); Canute died in the abbey, though buried in England's capital, Winchelsea. So wealthy were the town's founders that it was said 'If the Abbess of Shaftesbury could marry the Abbot of Glastonbury their heir would own more land than the king.' The last abbess was Elizabeth Zouch, who signed the deed of surrender to the king (or rather to his jackal, Thomas Cromwell) on 23 March 1539, so bringing to an end nearly 700 years of religious and historical continuity on this one spot.

But the town had long before emerged as an

Gold Hill, Shaftesbury, graphically illustrates the fact that the town is built on a high spur of rock. The cobbles were recently restored at a cost of £10,000.

independent entity and commercial centre with the charter granting the first market in 1260. It had two MPs until 1832, and returned one as late as 1884: it was not until the pernicious Local Government Act of 1974 that it lost the borough status Alfred the Great had given it about the year 880.

The late eighteenth and early nineteenth centuries gave the town a remarkable distinction, and a considerable fillip to its commercial life, for it became the junction of five turnpike roads. It was perfectly possible to leave London for a day's outing to Shaftesbury for the London–Devonport mail coach stopped at the Grosvenor Arms at 6.30 am, and returned there at 7.20 pm. Fortunately for posterity, the railway passed the town by, virtually bringing development to an end until road transport again dominated.

All the coaches stopped at the Grosvenor Arms, today a comfortable hotel which still shows its ancestry, and in one of whose rooms is an outstanding, indeed, a unique example of nineteenth-century woodcarving, the Chevy Chase sideboard. At first glance this massive piece of furniture seems to be an unusually well-preserved piece of German sixteenth-century work. It was, in fact, produced by a nineteenth-century Newcastle man, Gerrard Robinson, the son of a blacksmith. It seems to have taken him at least five years, between 1857 and 1862, and may have been commissioned by the Duke of Northumberland for his vast castle in Alnwick. For whatever reason, it never went to Alnwick and in 1919 was bought at auction for £140 by the landlord of the Grosvenor. Periodical attempts are made by Newcastle Corporation to acquire it, but it remains a southern trophy.

The tiny town's tiny museum is a triumph of civic self-help. Originally a doss-house (though in fact physically a delightful building set in a small garden), it is run entirely voluntarily and reflects local life and customs in a way that would do credit to a professional organization. Pride of the collection is the mysterious Byzant, an ornament decorated with ribbons, jewels and feathers which figured prominently in a major local custom. The town, on its great cliff, lacked water and a bargain was made with a local lord of the manor, allowing the townsfolk to descend and take water from certain lowland springs. An annual ceremony developed in which the mayor and burgesses would descend to the springs, bearing the Byzant and carrying gifts for the lord of the manor.

The mysterious Byzant. This extraordinary object figured in the annual ceremony in which the people of Shaftesbury descended the plain to receive water rights.

The museum is also notable for its collection of Dorset buttons, whose manufacture was once the town's major industry, attracting buyers to its market from all over the county. And on the main Salisbury road out of Shaftesbury is one of those anomalies which are the delight of English towns: an Anglican monastery, now a modern hotel.

THE HEART OF ENGLAND

AMERSHAM, BUCKINGHAMSHIRE

'Eahlmund's estate' *Anglo-Saxon*
Population: 17,464 *Market:* Tuesday, Friday

SOME regions of England not only transcend their administrative borders, no matter how ancient these may be, but also acquire a social significance of their own. The Chilterns is one such. Geologically they form a single high chalk ridge extending from Dorset to Norfolk. In practice, the name tends to be limited to the range from the Thames up into Bedfordshire. Unlike the neighbouring Cotswolds, there is no strong unifying factor about the landscape, or the towns and villages composing it. Lack of water is the major single characteristic of the region and this, in turn, accounts for the relative sparseness of development. Sparse, that is, until the twentieth-century boom in rail, and then road transport, when much of the area exploded into the very worst form of subtopian development.

Amersham escaped this – but only just. In the heyday of railway development the Metropolitan Railway Company brought their agency of mass transportation – the most potent cause of urban explosion – to the top of a hill barely a stone's throw from the old town. So proud were they of their achievement that, in the copious poster-advertizing that followed they dubbed Amersham-on-the-Hill 'Metroland'. The inevitable happened to Amersham-on-the-Hill as a tiny hamlet was transformed into a commuter-belt. There were one or two compensations. Station Road, linking the two Amershams, is rather more distinguished than most of its kind. Leading off it is a lane called High and Over whose houses, designed on the principles enunciated by Le Corbusier, were hailed on their appearance in the 1930s as an architectural breakthrough.

The 'mother town' is today the tip of a very large, roughly triangular development at whose other two corners are Little Chalfont and Chesham Bois. And, with all this immense pressure behind it, the fact that the old town has preserved its heart intact is

Amersham retains

52

remarkable. The little River Misbourne flows companionably beside the High Street, sometimes dodging out of view, sometimes adding to the townscape as at the Old Mill House. Dominating the market square is the red brick Market Hall, gift of a wealthy local family, the Drakes, in 1682. County, town and market halls, all following a roughly similar design, appeared in a number of towns over the following decade. Ten of them were built, in counties as far apart as Norfolk and Surrey, in a little over five years, springing less from necessity, one suspects, than from the same kind of civic pride that spattered England with tower flats in the 1960s. But Amersham's hall enhanced the town, a fine building set on arches in the traditional manner. A market charter had been granted in 1200 and brought very considerable trade to the town: 'A right praty market town on Fryday', that industrious traveller John Leland recorded.

He also noted that its one street 'was well buildyd with tymber'. The modest prosperity of the town led its wealthier citizens to follow the universal

its remarkably rural aspect in a heavily developed commuter area.

The King's Arms, one of Amersham's major coaching inns now stripped of its eighteenth-century façade to show its fifteenth-century structure.

finest funerary monuments in the Chilterns, those of the Drake family. Local squires for over 300 years, they gave the town its handsome row of almshouses. Their presence must have been very evident in Amersham for they not only owned most of the town, represented it in parliament as MPs and in heaven as vicars, but also lived in a vast Palladian mansion, Shardeloes House, which is still a major feature of the town. Robert Adam designed the exterior, James Wyatt the interior, and though it is now split up into separate residences its grounds still form a green backdrop to the town, a barrier against suburban sprawl in a vulnerable area.

ELIZABETH
Daughter of JOHN RAWORTH Esq.
Wife of W.M DRAKE Esq.
Born the 1.st of August 1725.
Deceased the 4.th of Feb.ry 1757.
Aged 32 Years.

The Drakes were Amersham's patron family, as evidenced by their grandiose memorials in the Drake Chapel of the Parish Church of St Mary.

Georgian custom of cladding the ugly timber in decorous brick. Most remain so hidden but, with considerable courage, the owners of the King's Arms stripped the brick façade to reveal an attractive fifteenth-century building beneath. Deciding what is the 'true' period for an ancient building is a perennial problem for conservationists, but there is little doubt that what must have appeared here as an act of vandalism at the time is a very distinct improvement. The gently curving High Street forms part of the old Aylesbury Road from London, its importance as a coaching route reflected by the number and nature of the inns that once all but lined it.

The church has felt the heavy hand of the Victorian 'restorer', responsible for almost as much destruction in his time as the 'developer' in ours. But it retains still that solid, low-profile appearance of churches in the Home Counties that is so much at variance with the soaring towers and spires of the north and east. It shelters what are probably the

BAKEWELL, DERBYSHIRE

'Baedecca's spring' *Anglo-Saxon*
Population : 3946 *Market :* Monday, including cattle

NOTHING is quite so dead as past fashion and, looking back from the twentieth century, it seems decidedly odd that our ancestors in the eighteenth and early nineteenth centuries should have expended so much time, energy and ingenuity in publicly laving their bodies in warmish water and gulping down the same unpleasant-tasting liquid in pursuit of health. But in Bakewell, at least, they were following an ancient tradition. The Romans, with that passion of theirs for bathhouses, gratefully established themselves here where generous springs of warm water rose from the limestone. By the Middle Ages the inevitable association of springs with miracles had taken place. The fifteenth-century chronicler, William of Worcester, identifies the River Wye, which rises near Buxton and passes through Bakewell, as the source of a holy well, attributing the usual medical miracles to it. William's Well, now in the recreation grounds just south of the town, and the so-called Great Well in Bath Street are the only surviving wells with any visible flow out of the half-dozen and more that once existed here.

Bakewell's spa had only a short-lived popularity, contributing little to the town's architecture compared with the spas at Bath, Buxton, Harrogate and elsewhere. The town's prosperity was founded firmly on its role as a trading place. Daniel Defoe, with that keen eye of his for business, remarked that 'Market towns being very thin placed in this part of the country ... have the better trade, the people generally coming twelve or fifteen miles to a market and sometimes much more.' Celia Fiennes, who visited the town on her way to Haddon Hall in 1697, had nothing to say about its baths, though she was an assiduous visitor of spas. It was, she thought, 'a pretty neate market town, it stands on a hill yet you descend a vast hill to it which you would think impossible to go down and by reason of the steepness and hazard of the Wayes – if you take the wrong turn there is no passing – you are forced to have guides as in all parts of Darbyshire'. It is sometimes difficult to get a clear picture of topography from Celia's breathless style, but here she is evidently remarking on the fact that Bakewell sits in a saddle some 400 feet above sea level, with hills towering more than 500 feet above it.

The town began life in the early tenth century as a Saxon burh, modelled on those established by King Alfred in the south a generation earlier. It flourished, judging by the very considerable number of Saxon funerary monuments discovered in the town and now preserved in the church. (So extensive were they that an even greater number than are now visible were built into the church walls.) The imposing Saxon cross in the churchyard, probably a century older than the town itself, also attests to the importance of Bakewell long before the Conquest. It not only figures largely in the Domesday Book, but its manor was sufficiently valuable to be bestowed upon the Conqueror's own illegitimate son. This was the William Peverell who built Haddon Hall, founding a short-lived dynasty there (see *Great English Houses* in this series). Over the following centuries the town passed in and out of the possession of successive lords of the manor, the last being the dukes of Rutland. It was not until 1921 that the Rutland estate disposed of its last interests in the town.

Bakewell gained a market charter as early as 1200, and a fourteenth-century lawsuit gives a fascinating insight into the economic value of a market to the lord of the manor. A certain John de Gernon levied a toll of 2d for every horse, 1d for a cow, and sheep and pigs were charged at four for 1d. The king's

North Church Street, Bakewell, with its distinctive houses fashioned with flint.

This is one of England's oldest town bridges, erected some time before 1539 to replace an even older bridge on the same site.

justices found that he was grossly over-charging and forced him to halve the toll. But even at that level it brought him in a substantial income in this agricultural district.

This is a rugged, northern town in that dark local stone which, though somewhat oppressive, weathers well. Undoubtedly the area of longest historical continuity is that around the Bath House. There is no documentary or archaeological evidence to back up the claim of Roman foundation, but it is unlikely that they would have ignored this major

Old Market Hall. Until 1890 it also served as Bakewell's Town Hall.

warm spring. The present building dates mostly from the late seventeenth century. The Rutland Arms in the square was built in 1804 on the site of the old White Horse Inn, evidence of the town's transient popularity as a spa. It was in the Rutland Arms, incidentally, that there took place that culinary accident which gave to the world what people will persist in calling the Bakewell 'tart' but which the locals correctly call a pudding.

In 1871 the lordly John Ruskin sneered at the coming of the railway which would allow 'every fool in Buxton to be in Bakewell in half an hour and every fool in Bakewell at Buxton'. His wish has at last been honoured, the railway has been dismantled, and the town in consequence is under heavy siege from road traffic. Ever since the 1930s there has been a debate about the routing of a bypass, but the only obvious course would be through the water meadows, a substantial part of the little town's charm. Two of Bakewell's river bridges are recognized as ancient monuments: the Bakewell Bridge in the town itself, dating from the early sixteenth century though widened on one side in the nineteenth, and the delightful Packhorse Bridge, built in 1694 and just wide enough for a horse (or a modern cyclist).

CIRENCESTER, GLOUCESTERSHIRE

'Roman town on the River Churn' *Anglo-Saxon*
Population : 15,622 *Market :* Friday *Cattle :* Monday, Tuesday

THE Romans, trying to get their tongues round the Celtic name 'Corin', called this town Corinium. The Saxons, who hesitantly began to take the place over about the year 577, added their own version of the Latin 'castrum' to the Celtic name and, in due course, bequeathed the whole confection to the English who modified it to Cirenceaster. There is a popular belief that the townsfolk pronounce their town's name as 'Sissister'. This was, indeed, the case from about the thirteenth to the nineteenth century. But with the advent of popular education this beautiful name began to be pronounced as spelt, as it is today.

But even if one were totally ignorant of the town's history, a glance at the map would provide a major clue. For Cirencester is the hub of an immense wheel whose almost arrow-straight spokes are formed by two of the great roads of Roman Britain, Ermine Street and the Fosse Way. Their intersection occurred at what was, after London, the biggest Roman city of all in Britain. Externally, there are far fewer Roman remains than in Colchester, Lincoln or York. A large, but shapeless amphitheatre on the far side of the bypass and a section of city wall and mound in the abbey gardens are the most important.

The head of Neptune from the famous Hunting Dogs mosaic floor, found in Dyer Street, Cirencester, in 1849.

Even the ground plan is not recognizably Roman, although the incomparable market place, reminiscent of the great Piazza del Campo at Siena, owes its site to the forum.

Altogether, not much to show for 500 years of Roman occupation. But the excellent Corinium Museum holds some of Britain's most perfect Roman mosaics. Ever since 1849, when the digging of drains brought to light the famous Hunting Dogs and Four Seasons mosaics, more and more Roman artefacts have been discovered, as often as not accidentally. Outstanding are the reconstructed tableaux, among them a Roman drawing room, that bring the whole period to life.

But if the best of Rome is under a museum roof, the most glorious part of the medieval town forms a backdrop to the workaday market. The best approach is from the north-east, first down the Fosse Way (now prosaically named the A429), then along Dyer Street where the mosaics were found. On turning

A limestone capital, probably from the free-standing column that once supported a statue of Jupiter in Corinium.

Cirencester, looking towards the market place. On the right is the Fleece

Inn, whose name is indicative of the industry that made the town's wealth.

Cirencester's Market Cross. Its older, traditional form should be compared with that of Chichester (see p. 145).

great abbey, the dominant religious body here. Indeed, so powerful was the abbot that, like the Pope in medieval Rome, he completely dominated the civic structure.

The abbey has long since disappeared, though its grounds form a welcome green oasis in the stone centre of the town. What the visitor now sees on entering the market place is a double feature: a soaring tower and, below it, an immense porch so large as to constitute a building in its own right, both built out of the same honey-coloured stone though separated by more than a century. In spite of its beauty, the porch serves a very practical purpose, the upper chamber serving as a town hall and the whole acting as a barrier between the church and the bustling life of the market place.

Cirencester has inherited that intangible gift of Rome which can only be called *urbanitas* – the ability of a place, no matter how small, to be a town rather than a village. It is a city in miniature and not simply an overblown village as are so many English towns. This is, admittedly, a characteristic of the stone towns of the area, but Cirencester's claim to be the Queen of the Cotswolds, regnant over towns not much smaller (or, for that matter much larger, if one considers the messy sprawl of Cheltenham) is undisputed. Street after street discloses architectural gems, most within the same colour range of Cotswold stone, though some with daring variations of texture and an occasional colour-wash for contrast.

But it is still a market town, mindful of the great trade in wool that generated the wealth that created the buildings. The first Monday in September sees the Sheep Fair, which originally traded mainly in the so-called 'Cotswold Lion', whose wool was the finest and most expensive in England. The most splendid inn in the town bears the name of the Golden Fleece and the largest coaching inn was The Ram. Currently, the town promotes one of the successful Cotswold Wool Weeks which, in addition to the usual fun fairs and pageants, includes demonstrations organized by the Gloucester Guild of Spinners, Dyers and Weavers. Since 1975 a group of local craftsmen have founded their own craftsmen's market, using the Victorian Corn Hall as a venue. There is, too, an industrial estate which infuses modern life into the ancient town, keeping its feet firmly on the ground, happily preventing it from becoming a self-conscious stage for antique shops.

the corner, the parish church bursts upon one's awareness without warning like a fanfare of trumpets.

This, one of the great wool churches of the Cotswolds (and, hence, one of the great churches of England if not Europe), began life humbly enough. The original building then stood at the gate of the

FARINGDON, OXFORDSHIRE

'Fern hill' Anglo-Saxon
Population : 4787 Market : Tuesday

ENGLISH rural names are often perversely grotesque with their 'Wallops' and 'Snorings' and 'Slaughters'. Occasionally, however, a name or phrase emerges of pure poetry and indubitably the 'Vale of the White Horse' is one such phrase.

Ideally, one should enter the vale from Swindon. The road clings to the side of the gentle but high hill that acts as boundary to the southern side. This is the hill that gives its name to the vale, and carved high above the village of Uffington is the extraordinary prancing white horse that was probably a Saxon tribal symbol.

From this vantage point, the whole rich vale can be seen; a quiet road leads on through the village of Uffington (the home of Tom Brown of 'Schooldays' fame) and up the other side of the vale to Faringdon.

Before the Norman Conquest it was an important town, the capital of this little rural kingdom tucked away between Swindon and Oxford. Alfred the Great had a palace here, and it was reckoned to be the third largest town in his kingdom of Wessex. It was here that the first true king of England, Alfred's son Edward, died in the year 924.

Strictly speaking, the town's name is Chipping Faringdon for the memorable King John in 1218 granted it the right to hold a weekly market, and the town promptly adopted the valuable prefix (Chipping was the Saxon term for market). Nothing remains of the Saxon palace; nothing remains of the twelfth-century castle, built by the Earl of Gloucester, or the Cistercian abbey built in the thirteenth century. But the intangible gift of King John has left

The market place with its Town House (market hall). Three large inns face onto this relatively small square of which one, The Crown, is just visible to the right.

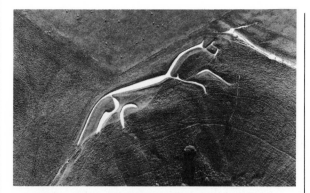

The White Horse, which gives its name to the vale, marks a Saxon tribal boundary.

its impress upon the town seven centuries later in the form of the exquisite market place. Its central feature – the Town House – is relatively new, having been built after the Civil War. Despite its grandiloquent name, it is what other towns would simply call a market hall. Butter, eggs and cheese were sold from the open ground floor, but the upper chamber was indeed used for the solemn purposes of a magistrate's room. It has had a varied history, for it served as a fire station at the turn of the century and currently its upper storey is used as the public library.

Three great inns face onto the market place, evidence of a very considerable trade. Of these The Salutation is probably the oldest. The name is almost certainly derived from the fact that it was the guest house of the monastery. But a remarkably unsympathetic extension in 1897, with the obligatory 'medievalization' of the time, has destroyed much of its architectural interest. The Bell is a delight, with that multiplicity of small wainscotted rooms that is one of the true characteristics of the English inn. But The Crown is superb. Although most of its façade is eighteenth century, the lower stone-mullioned windows are at least four centuries older. And in the great courtyard is one of the few surviving Elizabethan open staircases leading up to what used to be the courtroom. There is, too, a judge's staircase leading to the robing room whence he entered the courtroom.

Faringdon is a prime example of a town which originally drew its lifeblood from the road system. Situated at the junction of five main routes, including the important Oxford–Cirencester road, flocks of people came to buy and sell at the town's markets: cattle were bought and sold at the monthly cattle markets and horses at the bi-annual fairs. The coming of the railway both increased trade for the town, and took some of the strain off the roads. But then, coincident with the increase of road traffic, came the closing of the railway and for nearly a quarter of a century the town was choked by traffic. The bypass, opened in 1979, again restored the town to its citizens and those who wanted to visit it, as opposed to merely using it as a staging post.

Faringdon is perhaps remarkable for being unremarkable, important because unimportant. No great wealth has poured into it at any one period, enabling its suddenly prosperous burgers to turn their modest homes into fashionable architecture. The town is therefore a mosaic of architectural styles, almost a model of what a small market town should be. Here and there are extravagances. The most notable is the extraordinary folly built by Lord Berners in 1936, almost certainly the last ever likely to be built. The most elegant is Faringdon House, built (or rather rebuilt, for it is on the site of the old manor house) for George III's long forgotten poet laureate, James Pye. But the place as a whole excels as a quiet, well-mannered example of a Berkshire market town, still famous for its dairy products and fine bacon.

Lord Berners's folly, built in 1936, probably the last extravaganza of its kind.

KNUTSFORD, CHESHIRE

'Canute's ford' *Anglo-Saxon*
Population: 13,675 *Market:* Saturday

PLACE-NAME science is full of traps. Even when the derivation of a town's name can be verified, there is no guarantee that it relates to the popular belief that made it famous. Undoubtedly there was a ford here, and very probably there was a local lord called Canute. But was he *the* Canute who supposedly defied the waves? Local legend insists that it was and will even point to a place on the seashore at the Wirral a few miles away as the spot where the incident took place. In the grounds of the curiously named Mockbeggar Hall is an ancient wooden seat traditionally known as Canute's Chair. But the whole legend smacks of pious interpolations and, in any case, 'Knut' was a very common Danish name.

Knutsford's far more impressive claim to fame is its ability to maintain its individuality within the gravitational pull of Manchester, less than 10 miles away, which like some vast amoeba has absorbed communities as old and as once distinct as Knutsford. Even towns like neighbouring Macclesfield, which have preserved their physical identity, have succumbed almost wholly to the mass produced domestic architecture of the twentieth century.

Cheshire has always been an anomaly among English counties. Defoe remarked: 'it is a county Palatine, its government distinct from any other and very particular', and put his finger on that aspect of it which was to have such long-term physical effects. 'There is no part of England where there are such a great Number of Families of Gentry.' Throughout the eighteenth and early nineteenth century, this gentry emparked the county, obliterating entire villages, diverting roads, creating in effect a social vacuum which was filled by the industrial expansion of the late nineteenth century. Town after town was first besieged, then fell, then was engulfed.

Knutsford survived and its centre, in essential details, is probably not too dissimilar from its appearance in the 1840s when Elizabeth Gaskell absorbed its atmosphere prior to immortalizing it as Cranford, that perfect embodiment of English small-town life.

Knutsford owes its stability to its life as a market town. The local lord, William of Tabley, granted it a charter in 1292 with the right to hold a weekly

Mrs Gaskell immortalized this little Cheshire town when she transformed it into 'Cranford', that stronghold of redoubtable maiden ladies.

market and a fair on the feast day of the patron saints, Peter and Paul, in June. Fairs were of immense value in establishing a community as a rural metropolis and until the seventeenth century Knutsford and Manchester were probably equals. Then, in the nineteenth century, Manchester exploded, measuring its population first in tens, then hundreds of thousands while Knutsford moved up decorously from around 2000 in 1800 to perhaps 4000 a century later.

The town is, effectively, in two parts – Nether and Over – and it was Nether Knutsford that was destined to develop into the town centre. But the early dichotomy remains in the street pattern, the town possessing two main streets connected by a warren of lanes and alleys, giving it a greater impression of urban density than its size would

The black and white timber houses of King Street in the heart of the town are characteristic of the region.

warrant. King Street is the locality to which the visitor gravitates. The beautiful black and white houses that are characteristic of the street are reminiscent of the town's great neighbour, Chester, and as in Chester the casual eye is hard put to detect which houses are original and which are nineteenth-century confections. Architectural exuberance found extreme expression in the extraordinary villas built on the edge of the town in the 1880s for the use of businessmen commuting to Manchester. One particular road, Legh Road, attracted Pevsner's incredulous attention as 'the maddest sequence of villas in all England'.

Local piety, combined with an admirable resistance to 'development', has maintained the atmosphere of Mrs Gaskell's novels, allowing the visitor to follow in her footsteps and enter in imagination those prim little parlours where the terrifying ladies of Cranford drank their endless cups of tea. She was brought up by an aunt at Heath (now Heathwaite House), a handsome brick building on what is now Gaskell Avenue, and when she died in 1865 she was buried in the Unitarian Chapel. (She describes it, lovingly and at length, in her novel *Ruth* – it had 'a picturesque and olde-world look for luckily the congregation had been too poor to rebuild it, or new-face it in George III's time'.) Elizabeth Cleghorn Gaskell was considerably in advance of her time in recognizing that a decent penury is essential to enlightened preservation.

The present-day citizens of Knutsford seemed to have been particularly grateful to the writer who brought fame to their quiet town. In 1907, on the 150th anniversary of her birth, they erected in King Street a tower in her memory, together with a bust of her, a plaque that portrays her in later life and a list of her works. The extraordinary King's Coffee House next door was also dedicated to her. It still has something of its Art Nouveau atmosphere, reminiscent of the time when it was the meeting place of literary celebrities, Galsworthy among them.

LEDBURY, HEREFORD & WORCESTER

'Fort on the broad river' Anglo-Saxon
Population: 3630 Market: Tuesday, Saturday Cattle: Tuesday

JUST outside Ledbury the land heaves itself up suddenly, dramatically, in the first of the great ridges of the Malvern Hills. And somewhere in those hills on a May morning about the year 1360 William Langland, a clerk, had his vision of 'a fair field full of folk' which, in due course, became one of the earliest and greatest narrative poems in the English language, *The Vision of William concerning Piers the Plowman.*

It seems entirely appropriate that the author of this quintessentially English epic, celebrating the English farm labourer, should have been born in this quintessentially English market town. Apart from the church, the oldest surviving buildings in the town would not have appeared until at least a century after his death in 1399, but the extraordinary sense of continuity in the little town elides the centuries. Langland's gentle ghost, one feels, might be surprised but certainly not put out by what has happened to Ledbury in the intervening years.

The town is the beneficiary of British Rail's capricious attitude to rationalization and it still has a halt. To alight at that halt on a drowsy summer's morning is to go back half a century and more – to the opening, perhaps, of an Ealing Studios' comedy. A rather dull road lined with neat, prim houses widens without notice and one is, abruptly, in Ledbury's market place. Black and white is the dominant livery, for immediately in front is the Market House, seemingly teetering on its spindly wooden legs (but it has been doing that ever since it was first built in 1617) and beyond is the splendid, arrogant façade of the Feathers Hotel. In the distance appear yet more great black and white

The Market House, built in 1617, is timbered in a herringbone pattern and stands on pillars of oak.

houses, once the homes of wealthy merchants, facing the market place where they had made their fortune.

But to understand Ledbury or virtually any medieval English town, it is necessary to go up a narrow street like Church Lane, half hidden by the market place. It is in excellent condition, now lovingly maintained, and apart from the lack of

The Market House, still in use as a market today, with the nineteenth-century clock tower behind.

smell this is what a small-town street must have been like until the eighteenth century or even later. The low, two-storeyed houses, jettying out overhead, crowd so close that neighbour can very nearly touch the hand of neighbour across the street. The lane underfoot is cobbled and most of the buildings that line the lane are timber framed. More than that, they are close enough to the observer, and in good enough condition for the carpenters' identification marks to be visible. These marks, in the form of Roman numerals, are particularly evident in the old grammar school, built between 1480 and 1520 and superbly restored in the 1970s. These dwellings were, in effect, pre-fabricated and the carpenters' marks ensured that the correct parts were placed together. The efficiency of this system is shown by the fact that the building, standing detached in its

very own small courtyard on the west side of the lane, has been moved at least twice in its long life, once from the High Street to a private garden and quite recently to the present site.

The lane frames, and leads up to the massive Church of St Michael and All Angels. There was a church here at the time of Domesday in 1086, a building quite out of proportion to the then tiny hamlet of 'Liedeberge', for it was the minster church serving a wide area, and not simply a local parish church. In the formative years of Ledbury, the affairs of church and town were inextricably tangled. The all-powerful Bishop of Hereford included Ledbury among his many homes, and, some time after 1100, built an attractive manor house near the church. His presence, and need for money, altered the physical shape of the town. In Saxon times Church Lane had formed one side of the triangular market place of Ledbury. The bishop, with a lively awareness of the income to be reaped from a market, obtained a charter from the king about the year 1122. Evidently the old Saxon market was not large enough or convenient enough so a new market place was laid out at right-angles to it, and this now forms the present market place. One of the results of this change was to turn Church Lane into a backwater, happily preserving it for posterity's delight.

The link between bishopric and town ended in 1583, but by then Ledbury was mostly in the form we would recognize today. Indeed, it is probable that sixteenth- and twentieth-century Ledbury resemble each other more closely that at any intervening period. After the Great Fire of London, timber-built towns throughout the country took a closer look at their building material. More and more houses were built in brick and, during the eighteenth century in particular, the relatively vulnerable, and also unfashionable open timberwork was either plastered or given a brick façade. In our own time, the fashion has returned for exposed timbers, frequently with deplorable results in modern suburban architecture. Even when the timbers are original and integral, removing the plaster from some old buildings is like stripping the flesh from a skeleton. In Ledbury, however, timber was used both decoratively and constructively and in stripping the plaster here (for example, from the group of houses numbered from 27 to 29A in the Home End which was done in 1978) an act of genuine restoration has been achieved.

Church Lane, the perfect example of a medieval street. The carpenters' marks on the timber buildings, which enabled them to be pre-fabricated, are still visible.

LICHFIELD, STAFFORDSHIRE

'Open land in the grey wood' *Anglo-Saxon*
Population : 25,600 *Market :* Friday, Saturday *Cattle :* Monday

ONE of the mysteries of urban history is why some towns are able to preserve their character and integrity while others, resembling them topographically and economically in many ways, have wholly succumbed to the onslaught of the nineteenth and twentieth centuries. Lichfield is surrounded by towns afflicted with urban elephantiasis: Coventry, Nottingham, Wolverhampton, Birmingham, Burton and Stoke, all have changed beyond recognition and mostly for the worst. Since World War II Lichfield has also experienced what is termed 'development' but its heart is still a recognizable city.

Like Durham, the town owes its origin to a saint, Chad, the first bishop of Mercia who came here supposedly for solitude in the late seventh century. A shrine had certainly been erected to him here by the year 700 and this became the nucleus of three successive cathedrals on the site. The present cathedral, with its remarkable triple spires delightfully named 'the Ladies of the Vale', was completed by the early thirteenth century but was very heavily damaged during the Civil War when it became the object of two sieges. Close to, it can be seen that

Dr Johnson's statue in the market place
of his native town faces
his birthplace.

much of the work is a Victorian restoration but so well done that, from only a short distance, the cathedral of St Chad bears its medieval form.

Saints seeking solitude usually chose unsalubrious places and Chad seems to have been no exception for Lichfield, as he would have seen it, consisted largely of a chain of swamps. These determined the future site of the city for when, about 1129, Bishop Roger Clinton began to lay out his new town, building had to take place on the far side of the swamps. In effect, they provided a barrier between city and cathedral, a provision of nature not to be despised in the turbulent Middle Ages. Subsequently, they were drained and transformed into two large lakes or pools with Minster Pool still between cathedral and town.

The three 'Ladies of the Vale' crown Lichfield's cathedral.
The present building is the third on the site of St Chad's
eighth-century shrine.

Stowe Pool and St Chad's Church. The pool, with its twin known as the Minster Pool, was formed when the swamps were drained.

The two halves of Lichfield – ecclesiastic and secular – have therefore had two different courses of development. Roger Clinton's layout is still visible in the street pattern, not as impressive or as widespread as at Salisbury or Bury St Edmunds, two other towns laid out by an ecclesiastic, but still clear enough. And in the centre of his layout is the market place which, in the eighteenth century, saw a dramatic (or, perhaps, melodramatic) form of filial piety when Dr Samuel Johnson stood bareheaded in the pouring rain as penance for his attitude towards his father.

Johnson was a Staffordshire man, speaking with a Staffordshire accent till the end of his life. And, like that other Midlander, William Shakespeare, he kept his roots in his home town though he made his money and fame in London. The house where he was born in 1709 is now a museum, its polished wood and hushed atmosphere so characteristic of such institutions. But the market place, with its two statues commemorating both Johnson and his leech-like biographer James Boswell, still flouri-shes. Lichfield, like Warwick, is currently turning its most famous son into a profitable industry but, like Stratford, somehow keeps its two lives apart so that it is still a living Midland market town, and not simply a showpiece.

A mixture of small but flourishing industries brought a balanced livelihood to Lichfield. The stagecoach era held it firmly in the economic web of the Midlands and even when they were superseded by the railway, a station came near enough to the town in 1837 to ensure its continual prosperity. But even now it is by no means clear why it was spared the industrial onslaught of the 1850s onward which transformed the village of Birmingham into a vast, blackened monster, and Nottingham into a nondescript sprawl. Indeed so wealthy is the town in historic buildings that among the 300 listed as of architectural interest or importance, a considerable number have found a new lease of life as shops or offices. Dr Johnson, with his feet so firmly placed on the ground, would have approved this pragmatic mixture of commercialism and sentiment.

MARSHFIELD, AVON

'Boundary land' *Anglo-Saxon*
Population: 1000 *Market:* Saturday

MARSHFIELD is a place which makes nonsense of our attempt to classify communities into towns, villages, or cities. Along with communities far larger, it was robbed of its identity by the 1974 Local Government Act and submerged into the surrounding District. But this has happened to towns with populations in their tens or even scores of thousands. Even Marshfield's staunch defenders and chroniclers, the local Women's Institute, are content to call it a village. Nevertheless, it has all the attributes of a town: the right to hold a weekly market and a bi-annual fair, first granted in 1266; a picturesque Town House, built in 1690, and civic regalia, including a mace from the time of Charles I and carried by the parish clerk. The number of inns – at least thirteen before World War I, three of which still prosper today – testify to its importance as a rural metropolis as well as an important point on a stagecoach route.

The inclusion of Marshfield in the present book might perhaps be regarded as a curiosity, but certainly not an anomaly for this small town demonstrates the ability of an urban community to preserve its distinctive stamp even when shrunk to almost half its size (its population was around 1700 a century ago). Rather like a seed, Marshfield retains all its potential within a limited compass. Recently a new estate of houses has been added, giving depth to the place, bringing in new life. Yet ancient traditions, like Boxing Day Mummers, are not forgot-

The dovecote, Marshfield. Doves and pigeons were kept not for their aesthetic, but for their food value.

ten; after nearly a century, this festivity was revived in 1931 and now draws great crowds.

The most dramatic approach to Marshfield, ascending the immense combe from Bath to the south, makes nonsense of the obvious interpretation of the town's name for there are few marshes in this kind of country 600 feet above sea level. In fact, it owes its name to the same factors that christened its opposite number to the north-east, Moreton-in-Marsh (see p. 72). The probable meaning of 'marsh' in this context is 'boundary', for the great ridge upon which it sits was the boundary between the Anglo-Saxon kingdoms of Wessex and Mercia. The contrast between north and south is almost theatrical, giving topographical substance to philological reasoning for the ridge is a boundary between totally different types of country: to the north flat, with dry-stone walls; to the south carved with the deep lush valleys and combes of Somerset.

The new bypass has brought great relief to the town but has somewhat obscured its geographical significance; the houses and inns naturally grew up along the road which, in time, became the main Bristol–London route. The lengthy High Street is lined with the solid grey-stone houses of well-to-do

The almshouse deeds with the civic mace, which dates from 1635.

The Boxing Day Mummers of Marshfield, dressed in their costumes of coloured paper. The mummers were revived in 1931.

merchants which, in the urban manner, form a solid front. Behind each is the narrow, elongated 'burgage' plot which, in areas of expansion, have long since been built over or shortened but here survive as a prime example of early town development. Owners of these plots would pay rent to the local lord, but were free to pursue activities other than farming, so contributing to the variety of trades in the embryonic town.

As with most Cotswold towns, wool was the basis of Marshfield's affluence but this eventually gave way to malting. In the eighteenth century there were at least eighty malt-houses, a fact demonstrated by the façades of the houses in the High Street for most were either rebuilt or refaced in this period of prosperity. The town is real and substantial enough, but there is a curious theatrical air about it as though the whole were a stage setting, or one of those Renaissance exercises in perspective. At the entrance to the town at the east end is a Georgian Gothick tollhouse and, opposite it, a handsome but somewhat forbidding range of almshouses built in 1612. (It is in front of the almshouses that the Mummers, dressed in their paper suits, finally enact their play of life and death having made their way from the market place.) From the almshouses the

long grey-stone street stretches into the distance until closed by a group of inns and houses on a sudden bend to the left. Half way along is the Town House, or Tolzey, about the same date as the great Catherine Wheel Inn alongside it but much smaller. It is nevertheless a distinctive building and it is odd that so self-respecting a town should have turned the entire ground floor of what was once their town hall into a public lavatory.

The market place is neatly tucked away where the road bends and is surrounded by some outstanding edifices: the National Schools, built in 1861, and still happily in use as a primary school; the church, rebuilt by the monks of Tewkesbury Abbey in 1471 and its attendant Georgian vicarage; a medieval barn and dovecote. The cattle market in Marshfield was once of considerable importance, growing so large that it was removed to an adjoining field, while the market place was given over to sideshows. As with so many other local markets it declined and disappeared altogether after World War II. But the tradition has been maintained by the Marshfield Women's Institute which determinedly keeps its own weekly market in the church hall, itself converted from an old barn largely through the efforts of the townsfolk.

MORETON-IN-MARSH, GLOUCESTERSHIRE

'Moor village by the boundary' *Anglo-Saxon*
Population: 2711 *Market:* Tuesday

THIS was the town which gave its name to one of the funniest radio shows of World War II – *Much Binding in the Marsh* – purporting to be the saga of a mythical and remarkably incompetent RAF station. But, as in so many English place names, nothing is quite what it seems. Like Marshfield, the nearest marsh must be many miles away, for this is a Wold town, over 400 feet above sea level. About a mile and a half outside the town on the way to Oxford there is an ancient boundary stone (to which Moreton's name relates), known as the Four Shires Stone for it marks the junction of Gloucestershire,

The Four Shires Stone, marking the meeting place of Gloucestershire, Warwickshire, Worcestershire and Oxfordshire, gives Moreton part of its name.

Warwickshire, Worcestershire and Oxfordshire. The name is, at the very least, 300 years old and the stone very much older for that indefatigable Puritan tourist, Celia Fiennes, remarked on it when she passed this way in 1697.

The town was created by and for the Fosse Way, that great artery of Roman Britain that carves its way from Lincolnshire to Wiltshire. This is immediately apparent as soon as one enters the town for it is, essentially, a development on both sides of the Way. Given its name, it must have come into existence during the Anglo-Saxon period, after the counties had been established, and the present nineteenth-century church is supposed to be on a Saxon site. Some of the older houses and inns also date from the sixteenth century or earlier. But, in general, Moreton-in-Marsh is an excellent illustration of a town developing through trade and industry for, compared with most of its Cotswold neighbours – Chipping Campden or Stow-on-the-Wold, for instance – it is an adolescent, being mostly eighteenth or nineteenth century.

The reason is simple. The wealth of Moreton's neighbours, which enabled them to build and expand and decorate themselves, was founded on wool. Moreton's prosperity was founded first on the weaving of linen, a trade which followed the declining wool industry, and was bolstered by the town's position on a major stagecoach route. Transport has undoubtedly provided most of Moreton's vitality. After the stagecoach, and before the coming of the railway, an ingenious engineer, William James, built a horse-drawn tramway from Stratford to Moreton in 1826. It was operating at least until 1864 when a correspondent on the magazine *London Society* described its curious method of operation: 'The journey was performed outside an ordinary railway carriage which had been adapted to the necessities of horse traction. Attached to the carriage in front was a platform on which the sagacious horse mounted when it had drawn our carriage up to the top of the incline, thus escaping being tripped up as we descended at a rattling good speed. When the carriage came to a stand, the horse dismounted and drew us along as before.' The railway proper came to Moreton in 1848. By one of the quirks of railway administration, it escaped the ferocious cuts of the 1960s known as the Beeching Axe; for no discernible reason, therefore, one can still travel by fast train from the heart of London to this small market town.

Most of the town's taverns and inns that once served stagecoach passengers have been upgraded to expensive tourist hotels. The White Hart took the name of Royal, claiming that Charles I stopped here in 1644. He may well have done for the inn is certainly of considerable antiquity. The floor of the now enclosed entrance hall is cobbled and was undoubtedly once the main drive into the inn courtyard. The beautiful Manor House Hotel, with its splendid garden, is probably sixteenth century in origin. There is evidence of a Tudor bear-baiting pit in the grounds and the house was once the home of a family of local gentry, the Creswyckes, the head of the family being knighted in 1663.

There are two major public buildings, the sixteenth-century curfew tower and the nineteenth-century Town Hall. This massive, rather clumsy structure, built in the local stone and style, was the gift of Lord Redesdale, father of the Mitford sisters. Built in 1887 to mark Queen Victoria's Golden Jubilee, it was originally open on the ground floor in the usual manner but the arches were later somewhat misguidedly filled in, creating its heavy ap-

Moreton-in-Marsh's Town Hall was the gift of Lord Redesdale, marking Queen Victoria's Golden Jubilee in 1887. The ground floor was originally open.

pearance. All in all, Moreton seems to have undergone the final stages of gentrification with a plethora of antique shops and gift shops, but appearances are misleading. There is a market each Tuesday, a lively affair that takes place in the widened section of the High Street that has been a market place for centuries. And it still clings jealously to its right to hold a fair twice yearly, in April and September, even though the attractions are now mainly mechanical or electronic. The Fosse Way continues to feed its child.

Moreton was created by, and for, the great Fosse Way. Here the ancient Roman road can be seen cutting through the town.

NEWARK-ON-TRENT, NOTTINGHAMSHIRE

'New work' *Anglo-Saxon*
Population: 24,091 *Market:* Saturday, Wednesday, Friday *Cattle:* Wednesday

THE 1974 Local Government Act extinguished the ancient governance of this Midland town. But it promptly formed a Charter Trusteeship whose prime purpose was 'to enable the mayoralty of the town to be preserved and the historic and ceremonial functions of the town to continue'. Thus, despite the flattening anonymity effected by this Act Newark continued to maintain those functions which are the essential outward signs of a community's character. They are today purely ceremonial and without powers, but one has a sneaking feeling that some day they may yet again come into their own.

This is all of a piece with a tough community which has endured siege, fire, plundering – and once disappeared altogether, if its place name is any evidence. It is unlikely that the town is of Roman

The soaring spire of Newark's parish church.

foundation, as was once believed, although it stood on the Fosse Way. After the Roman withdrawal, Angles established a community here but this was so totally destroyed by the Danes that it had to be built completely anew, the 'new work'. The town was in the Danelaw, that part of England permanently ceded to these ferocious but energetic new immigrants, and their influence lives on, too, in Newark's street names. Cartergate, Kirkgate, Appletongate and the like are common in the East Midlands, the word 'gate' meaning 'way' or 'road'.

The town was one of the staunchest defenders of Charles I during the Civil War. Indeed, the war started hereabouts for Charles passed through the town on his way to that disastrous 'raising of the Standard' in Nottingham in August 1642. The Cromwellians besieged the town three times: in 1643, in 1644 (with 8500 men, 13 guns and 2 massive mortars), and finally in 1646. Even then the town refused to surrender until ordered by the king. The garrison marched out on 9 May and, two days later,

Dance of Death, Newark. Most murals of this subject were inspired by the fourteenth-century Black Death.

Newark Castle was ordered to be 'slighted' or destroyed after the Civil War, but the stupendous river frontage remained, together with the gatehouse where King John died.

the citizens were ordered to destroy the castle that had been at the centre of resistance.

The 'slighting' or destruction of royalist castles was a commonplace after the war, but not always fully carried out. At Newark the river front survives, creating a spectacular approach to the town; so, too, does part of the tower and the handsome gatehouse in which King John was brought to breathe his last in 1216.

The charter which Elizabeth I granted the town gave it the very valuable privilege of holding a fair – the May Fair. This evolved into the Newark agricultural show in 1868, and in 1959 was merged into the Newark and Nottingham show. This is now held on the edge of the town, but the great market place once known as the Market Stede still pursues its function in the town centre. The inns which sprang up to cater for visitors still play a lively role in the market place. W. E. Gladstone used the Clinton Arms as his headquarters for his first election battle here (he was Newark's MP from 1832 until 1846) and Byron stayed in the same inn on his business visit to the town. The great White Hart has recently been restored to its past role in this town's social life. Instead of selling only alcoholic beverages and, in consequence, remaining sullenly closed outside the eccentric British licensing hours, a wide range of food and drink is sold and it is now a civilized centre for both adults and children throughout the day.

There are a considerable number of major historic buildings apart from the castle and the great inns of the market place. The parish church of St Mary Magdalene is a showpiece of the Midlands. The ever memorable Lady Godiva gave the church and manor to the monastery of Stow, near Lincoln, in 1055 but the main body of the church is well preserved, its structure dating from the twelfth to the fourteenth century. The Markham Chapel, built in 1505, has two murals depicting the 'Dance of Death'. This kind of memento mori was very common after the Black Death of the 1350s but this is an unusually late representation of the sixteenth century. Cromwell is supposed to have used the church as stables, a charge frequently made but less often sustained. His horses certainly did far less damage here than the deliberate inconoclasm practised in East Anglia. The Governor's House in Stodman Street is a superb late sixteenth-century half-timbered building (spoiled, as is only too common, by shops insensitively carved out of the ground floor), and it was in this house that Charles had the celebrated row with Prince Rupert which led to the prince's loss of his post as general. And in Newark's regalia is an excellent example of that ritualized alcoholism which underpinned so much of English municipal life. This is the great 'Newark Monteith', a silver bowl for the washing of wine glasses, given to the Corporation in 1689.

Newark's market place is in the tradition of the 'forum' – a large

open area lined with buildings of great architectural variety.

STOW-ON-THE-WOLD, GLOUCESTERSHIRE

'Market on the Wold' Anglo-Saxon
Population : 1677 Market : suspended

FOR at least 2000 years, the great Fosse Way has been the scene of intense activity along the length of its diagonal route across England. Most Roman roads pierce the hearts of the towns they serve: at Stow-on-the-Wold, the town turns its back on the Fosse Way, creating a fortress-like appearance for the windows of the massive, grey-stone buildings that overlook the road are small, and doorways are few. Certainly it is a blessing for Stow today as traffic is heavy, intense and incredibly noisy. But why did the original builders of the town draw its skirts away from a major highway whose very busyness would have been welcome?

Whatever the reason, this uncharacteristic action has created a haven for its citizens and a delight for travellers. From Lincoln to Moreton-in-Marsh to Stow, the venerable Fosse Way has become a very modern trunk route. But it is an exhilarating road as it dips and swings through the beginning of the Cotswolds, climbing at last the hill which is crowned by Stow. For here again the little town is something of an anomaly among its peers: English towns prefer to snug themselves down in valley bottoms and alongside rivers but Stow has followed the Italian pattern and chosen a hill top. It did not even have the justification of Shaftesbury in Dorset,

The beautiful, honey-coloured stone, used for both public and private buildings, gives this Cotswold town a handsome unity.
The cross stands in the large market place.

Stow market place is, in effect, divided into two by a group of buildings in the centre. The ancient stocks are in the quieter eastern section.

or Durham for instance, for it was never a fortified town.

Leaving the Fosse Way one is plunged immediately into the life of the town. Like all the stone towns of the Cotswolds it is solidly built in continuous terraces. This density of development creates a remarkably urban feeling for so small a place. Stow exhibits one of the most dramatic small-town vistas in England: the narrow winding lane called Church Street that leads off the Fosse Way takes the traveller, without warning, into an immense open space, the market place, which was the venue for the great horse markets that created Stow's fame and modest wealth. But that first glimpse of a stone symphony, infinitely subtle in its variation of shades from grey to brown to gold, is vulgarized by the dozens of gaudily-coloured cars parked permanently in the square. It is as though a pop song had been inserted into a Bach cantata.

Some of Europe's most perfect small towns are built in the bleakest countryside as though the citizens were turning inward from hostile or indifferent surroundings. Such a factor seems to have been at work in Stow. The town began as an Iron Age settlement, ringed around by earth ramparts in order to keep cattle penned in. This ancient pattern is still visible from the south where a green embankment rises from the valley bottom to be crowned with a line of modern houses which should look incongruous but, oddly, reinforce the picture of an early hill-top village. Odds and ends of archaeological discoveries – a Stone Age axe, Roman coins and tiles – establish the town's great age. But its affluence came in the Middle Ages with the marketing of the sheep whose wool made first the Cotswolds', and then England's, prosperity. One of the three roads leading off the Fosse Way is named, appropriately, Sheep Street and leading off this are a number of narrow alleyways known locally as 'tures'. Where they leave Sheep Street the tures are wide enough for two, or even three people to pass, but where they enter the market place it is only just possible for one adult to get through. It is presumed that these tures were specifically designed to enable sheep to be counted and, indeed, their funnel shape would allow this practice perfectly. Certainly, at the peak of Stow's prosperity, some 40,000 sheep would have exchanged hands at the market.

But it was the twice annual fair which made Stow's name. The monks of the abbey of Evesham in 1476 obtained a charter allowing them to hold a

One of the two wells, both half a mile outside the town, which were the sole source of water until the 1860s.

fair in May and October. Sheep, hops and cheese were the main commodities until the nineteenth century when horse trading became more important. It is a curious fact that dealing in horses seems to attract a dubious class of dealer, in much the same way as the modern trade in second-hand cars. Not far from the market place is a narrow lane where, it was common knowledge, worthless horses bought at knockdown prices would be doctored, taken back and sold at a higher price. A famous Stow story is told of a farmer who sold his worn-out hack for £10 in the morning, got drunk during the day, and unwittingly bought back the doctored beast for £30 in the evening.

The Stow horse fair is a sturdy example of survival over the vast technological changes which have driven the horse as a working beast off the farm, and the bi-annual fairs bring back something of the town's working past. In the main, Stow-on-the-Wold is today a tourist town with antique shops and hotels outnumbering by far workaday shops and businesses. But the stoutly-built inns and taverns defy all but the most dedicated refinement. About half a mile outside Stow is a sober reminder of the harshness of life here, almost within living memory. Built on top of a hill, Stow has no natural water supply. Down the street appropriately known as Well Lane are two stone-built wells. The upper well has certainly been in use since the mid sixteenth century, and both were in regular use until the 1860s. Until that date, the women of Stow had the choice either of buying water brought from the wells by watercart at a farthing a bucket, or of toiling up the hill with their own buckets. It is an idyllic walk for an unburdened visitor on a pleasant day. For a weary woman in winter it must have been a daily purgatory.

WARWICK, WARWICKSHIRE

'Farm by a weir' Anglo-Saxon
Population : 21,936 Market : Saturday Cattle : Wednesday

THE name of Warwick echoes sonorously in English history. Every school-child knows the name of 'Warwick the King-maker', otherwise Richard Neville, earl of Warwick, who had so many fingers in so many pies before being killed at the Battle of Barnet in 1471. But 'Warwick' was a title borne by three other great dynasties, as well as the Nevilles – Beauchamp, Dudley and Greville.

Some of these personalities can be seen, fashioned in marble or metal, in the exquisite Beauchamp Chapel in St Mary's Church, probably the foremost examples of funerary monuments in all Britain, not excluding London. The chapel was built (at a cost precisely calculated as £2783 19s 2½d) over some twenty years by Richard Beauchamp. He was the Earl of Warwick who hounded Joan of Arc to her death and he lies now, in silver-gilt splendour, on top of his tomb, his eyes devoutly fixed on the Virgin Mary on the wall at his feet. His dominant tomb is between two of the Dudleys – Ambrose, earl of Warwick, and Robert, earl of Leicester. Robert was host to Elizabeth I at one of the most prodigal extravaganzas even Tudor England had seen when the queen visited him at nearby Kenilworth Castle. But he also founded the almshouse for twelve veterans of the queen's wars which, known as Lord Leycester's Hospital, is today one of the town's outstanding architectural showpieces.

The arrogant demands of an eighteenth-century earl, together with the no less arrogant demands of twentieth-century traffic have somewhat shifted the town's axis. Warwick began life down by the river, at the place now called Bridge End which would presumably have been the site of the original 'farm by a weir'. There are still remains of the ancient bridge which crossed the River Avon here under the very shadow of the enormous castle. In 1788 the earl obtained an act of parliament which allowed him to build a new bridge upstream and close its predecessor. The new, elegant, stone bridge (the work of a local mason, William Eborall) spans the river in one superb arch and now carries a modern road. It was probably during this major operation that most of the town's southern wall was demolished, leaving the East Gate isolated. The town, on the whole,

The splendid Beauchamp Chapel in the Church of St Mary. The central tomb is that of its founder, Richard Beauchamp, earl of Warwick.

benefited from the draconian operation. The fact that traffic could circulate round the old fifteenth-century town gate undoubtedly saved it, and the medieval chapel on the gateway itself was actually rebuilt at this time.

The road alignments have preserved two exceptional localities: Bridge End, and its companion piece Mill Street on the other side of the river. Both are now cul-de-sacs and look much as they would have done before the eighteenth-century realignment of the river crossing. The grounds of the castle, as finally laid out in the eighteenth century, occupy probably half of the historic core of the town but, curiously, although the castle itself is enormous, its position down by the river means that

Caesar's Tower, Warwick Castle, beneath which passed the ancient road bridge.

Lord Leycester's Hospital, Warwick. Founded by the Earl of Leicester as a hospital for old soldiers, this attractive example of Tudor architecture later became an almshouse.

the visitor to the town can be quite unaware of its presence. It is only from the river itself (and particularly from the bridge) that one can obtain the view of what seems to be an archetypal medieval fortress: the great towers with their romantic names – Guy, Caesar, Clarence – some of them reflected in the tranquil Avon, and the endless ranks of windows with their Gothic arches.

The castle earned considerable notoriety in the 1960s when its owner, Lord Brooke, sold off its art treasures one by one finishing, logically if bizzarely, by selling the castle itself to Madame Tussauds for £1.5 million. The Greville family seems to have been as indignant as the general public. Yet the castle has undoubtedly benefited from its new ownership. The restrained use of waxworks in the residential area has actually provided a lively insight into the working of a castle in Edwardian England and this new investment has enabled the enormous building to be kept in apple-pie order.

Warwick is one of those fortunate towns where a modicum of industry not only provided it with a modest prosperity, but also prevented it from becoming merely a showpiece – and still does. The opening of the canal from Birmingham in 1792 triggered off industrial development in the first decades of the nineteenth century. Among the relics of this period are the gasworks, a building combining very considerable charm with, until recently, functionalism. Warwick has always had this ability to place a building that truly reflects its age happily among others of greater antiquity. Even the twentieth century has, for once, made a positive contribution in the shape of the new County Council offices. The seventeenth and eighteenth centuries are particularly well represented, ranging from St John's House, built in 1626, on the site of a twelfth-century hospice to the Shire Hall, built in the 1750s and restored in 1948.

The Market Hall, built in 1670, originally stood on open arches, the space beneath being used for market stalls. It was railed off in the nineteenth century and now, with the entire ground floor bricked in, serves as the County Museum. But the life of the market still goes on around it. Like most northern and eastern towns, Warwick's market place is a distinct locality in the heart of a complex of streets, and the small shops that flourish around it are, indeed, the lineal descendants of the original market stalls.

THE EASTERN COUNTIES

BOSTON, LINCOLNSHIRE

'St Botolph's town' *Anglo-Saxon*
Population: 26,425 *Cattle Market:* Wednesday, Saturday

NOTHING, but nothing, prepares the first-time visitor for the full impact of the interior of the church which gave this town its name.

Descending from the relatively high lands of the Wolds to the north, the traveller will have seen the Stump (as the church's tower is called) from a good

Some of those Pilgrim Fathers who were later to embark on the Mayflower *were imprisoned in the Guildhall, the gates of which display this coat-of-arms.*

Shodfriars' Hall, built in 1874, is an excellent copy of a fifteenth-century building with elaborately carved plaster work. It takes its name from the old friary.

15 miles away. The vertical smudge grows taller, its outline clearer during the journey across the intervening flat lands of the Fens. Unlike most English churches, it does not disappear as one enters the town, coyly hiding behind adjacent buildings. Instead, that ugly-named Stump emerges in its true shape as a graceful, fretted tower soaring high above its neighbours. Begun about 1430 (over a century after the church itself) and taking some ninety years to build, the vast structure is quite hollow save for the belfry. At certain angles and at certain times of the day one can look right through it. And this graceful giant, seemingly made of filigree, forms the tower of a parish church that is as big as a cathedral and commensurately rich inside. It is not without significance that the architect of the Stump was the same Reginald of Ely who built that supreme example of the medieval chapel at King's College, Cambridge.

Boston Stump, the great tower of St Botolph's Church, is 272 feet high. A third of Lincolnshire is visible from its lantern which towers over the typical East Anglian market place where St Botolph's fair is held in May.

Some time about the year 350 a monk (and later saint) called Botolph obtained permission from the King of the South Angles to build a monastery on one of the innumerable islands that rose a few feet above the Fens. The Danes destroyed this, as they destroyed so much else on this vulnerable coastline, in 870, but the memory of 'Botolph's town' persisted and a new community came into being not far from the original site. Two centuries later it was still such a poor little place that the Conqueror's tax gatherers did not bother to record its existence in the Domesday Book. The tremendous stimulus provided by the Norman invaders, however, thrust this small settlement into the position of one of the major ports of the country – in 1289 it was paying one-third more in customs duties than London.

The sea was to be the source of the town's wealth, for through this port on the North Sea passed much of the wool that was, in turn, creating the wealth of England. The members of the Hanseatic League, with that keen eye of theirs for profitable investment, established their steelyards and warehouses in the town. There were ups and downs: plague, inundation of the sea, the silting up of the river which was the town's road to the world beyond. Each was overcome. In the nineteenth century a direct outfall to the Wash permitted large vessels to come upstream, ensuring the success of the docks whose construction was commenced in 1881. They still play a vital role in the town's economy, handling around one million tons of goods a year. And some idea of Boston's importance as a market town is gained from the size of the market place. It is immense and, like those in most East Anglian towns, is a clear-cut space specifically set aside for the purpose – a forum in fact – though, curiously, none of the town's important buildings actually abut onto it. In the third week of May a particularly raucous fair drives out the usual stall holders.

The town's situation, in due course, also ensured its emotional and historical link with what was to be the United States of America. In September 1607, a group of religious dissidents (later known as the Pilgrim Fathers) boarded a ship for Holland. They were betrayed by the captain, arrested and thrown into the cells at the Guildhall while awaiting trial. Twenty-three years later a more successful expedition actually reached New England, establishing a settlement which, with an odd sense of piety, was named Boston. In July 1938, perhaps the most famous American Bostonian of all, the father of the future President Kennedy, designated a room in the beautiful seventeenth-century Fydell House for the use of visitors from Boston's name-sake in Massachusetts.

Fydell House stands immediately next door to the Guildhall, one of those happy contrasts in which the historic towns of England excel. For where Fydell House is the perfect classic building, its proportions carefully planned, the Guildhall is simply a long, barn-like structure which has just grown over the centuries. It was built for one of the five guilds of the town in 1450 and was taken over as a town hall after being sequestrated in 1545. From then until 1887 it formed the very heart of the town's civic life. Although it is entirely without plan, there is a homely grandeur about the place, achieved perhaps by the use of broad oak beams to panel the brick walls. The kitchen is intact, as is the banqueting room (that indispensable venue of a medieval council) and the council chamber itself. The Guildhall is used today as a museum and the way in which the artefacts are displayed, as though just put down by their last user, adds to the feeling of a building still lived in. Most poignant of all, perhaps, are the two cells, still with their grills, still with their lockers and oaken benches on which many a despairing wretch must have tossed sleepless nights, as well as a handful of courageous men whose descendants were, in the fullness of time, to found America.

Fydell House, built in 1726, perpetuates the link with Boston, Massachusetts, for transatlantic descendants of the Pilgrim Fathers have a room here reserved for their use.

GRANTHAM, LINCOLNSHIRE

'Granta's estate' Anglo-Saxon
Population: 30,084 Market: Saturday Cattle: Thursday

GRANTHAM'S High Street forms part of the Great North Road, the road that for centuries has been one of England's major highways. Sadly, the High Street is a product of the 1960s when 'developers', backed by the 'planners' who were supposed to restrain them, were gutting historical towns in order to 'maximise site values'. The traveller might well be tempted to go straight past – and that would be a very great pity indeed. For, just off this drab thoroughfare, is one of England's great parish churches in a medieval townscape, a delightfully insouciant Guildhall, and a market that takes over the town centre on a Saturday.

One aspect in favour of the present High Street is that its gimcrack construction will barely last a generation before requiring total renewal. And Grantham seems particularly good at entirely changing its skin. When Celia Fiennes visited the town in 1697 she found it 'all built with stone'. With few exceptions, there is scarcely any evidence of stone today: the town's major buildings, both private and public, were substantially rebuilt or, at the very least, refaced in brick during the eighteenth century.

The town has no identifiable centre, possibly because it began life as a linear town, growing up on either side of a great highway, but also perhaps because its natural centre, the market place, was moved. Market and church once shared the same locality, but when the church was extended in 1280 the market was moved to its present site on the other side of the highway.

The market place is surrounded by potentially attractive, but currently dilapidated buildings. Yet the dilapidation is itself an attraction for most bear the form outside (and many inside) of the small-town shop a generation and more ago. In the centre is the graceful market cross which has had a remarkably peripatetic existence. It was erected within a decade of the market establishing itself here and remained until 1779, when the lord of the manor removed it. The potency of the market cross image was well demonstrated by the storm of protest that this action created, a storm before which the manorial lord was forced to bow. But it was removed

again in 1886, only to be replaced, by the successor of the same feudal lord, with a clumsy obelisk. Again the townsfolk protested and in 1914 the original cross was replaced. Considering the cavalier manner in which historical artefacts were treated until the present century, the survival of the cross while in storage is remarkable. Not far from it is an even more impressive relic, the dignified stone conduit or cistern which was built in 1597, and was used for watering horses certainly until World War II.

Two great inns redeem the dull High Street, the curiously named Angel and Royal and The George. The façade of the Angel has the same distinction as the George and Pilgrim at Glastonbury and was probably built about the same time although the inn itself goes back to 1213, established as a medieval hostelry by the Knights Templar. Unlike the Glastonbury inn, however, the splendid stone façade is the only early part that remains, the rear of the building having been substantially changed to

A detail from the Angel and Royal Inn, so-called after the visit of the Prince of Wales in 1866.

Kingdom, next to that of Salisbury Cathedral'. Since 1781 it has been the home of a flourishing society of bell-ringers. Scott was called upon to carry out the massive restoration programme that was considered virtually mandatory throughout the Victorian era, doing rather less damage than most of his fellow architects. This is still, essentially, a medieval church whose modern accessories simply

Grantham market place. Its slender, graceful cross is one of the oldest in England.

The Victorian Guildhall, built in 1867. Newton's statue stands in front of the Guildhall in his native town.

match the demands of the eighteenth-century coaching trade. The room where Richard III signed Buckingham's death warrant in 1483 is still extant, though much changed. The bow windows on the ground floor, with their superb carvings would, however, still be recognized by King Richard. Over the arch outside is the great gilded Angel which gave the inn its name: the sycophantic suffix was added in 1866 when the Prince of Wales (later Edward VII) stayed at the inn – an indication, at least, of its comfort and status. Further along the High Street The George reverses the picture, for the eighteenth-century façade fronts a much older building, parts of which can still be traced. Dickens brought his hero, Nicholas Nickleby, to this inn on his journey to the Dotheboys Hall.

The Parish Church of St Wulfram still sits in its complex of medieval streets, gaining authority from its authentic surroundings whilst conferring dignity upon them. The immense tower with its soaring spire ($202\frac{1}{2}$ feet high) was the very first of the great Lincolnshire towers that dot the county like so many cathedrals. Finished in 1280, it was described by George Gilbert Scott as 'the finest in the

point up its historical continuity. John Hayward's superb stained glass windows, for example, are uncompromisingly modern while fitting happily into their early English setting.

And a little further along from the church, is an honest, delightful piece of Victoriana – the Guildhall. It was built in 1867, before the inventiveness and exuberance of the early Victorians had ossified into pomposity. It is probably not a satisfactory building to work in and must present real problems of maintenance. But it provides a much-needed bubble of lightheartedness in the twentieth-century vista of the High Street.

KING'S LYNN, NORFOLK

'King's pool' *Anglo-Saxon*
Population: 33,340 *Market:* Tuesday, Saturday *Cattle:* Monday, Friday

THIS is the very archetype of a market town, for the two great central squares around which the town's life revolves are known as Tuesday Market (where, not surprisingly, a market is held every Tuesday) and Saturday Market.

Tuesday Market is, quite simply, superb – a huge balanced square ringed round with great inns. The best time to see it is on a Monday evening, before the market arrives and after the cars that sadly clutter the square by day have been driven off. Then one can see at a glance the remarkable harmony that has somehow emerged between buildings whose erection has been separated by, perhaps, centuries, the whole now forming one vast hall, its roof the sky itself. Among the inns is the The Mayden's Head (possibly named after Elizabeth I), headquarters in its time of the artillery company that manned the guns at St Anne's fort. 'We installed our brother Johnson Captain of Trinity Hall Ward, after dis-

secting plum pudding and roast beef with our new scimitar', one of their Minutes reads. Almost adjoining it is the magnificent Duke's Head, the work of the same architect who created the Customs House. Both inns have been somewhat refined but on Tuesdays, when the market comes to roaring, rattling life, the inns again come into their own.

Saturday Market is smaller, less formal, and perhaps even more spectacular with its bold use of the local material, flint. Here was the original site of the town – Bishop's Lynn, as it was known until the sixteenth century. For this is yet another of England's towns with an ecclesiastical foundation. Herbert de Losinga, bishop of Norwich, founded a priory here between two tiny tributaries of the River Ouse in 1101. The great church of St Margaret's that dominates the square is a very substantial relic of the priory. It is also a remarkable example of the way a building can survive the most adverse events:

Tuesday Market, one of the most perfect examples of the planned market place in England. The Duke's Head Inn (the pink central building) was built by Henry Bell.

King's Lynn, as befits a town with two centres, has two guildhalls. This is Holy Trinity Guildhall in Saturday Market, which became the town's seat of government.

over the centuries the marshy Norfolk soil has settled, putting heavy stresses on the church so that there now seems to be scarcely a perpendicular line in the whole building.

Towards the end of the twelfth century, the town expanded beyond the little Purfleet stream to form what is now the Tuesday Market area. King Street forms the link between these two centres, and marking the junction is the building that has virtually become the badge of King's Lynn – the Customs House, built in 1683. This is the heart of the town, the area by the river which generated commerce. That great guild of German merchants, the Hansa, settled in King's Lynn sometime during the thirteenth century and maintained the link until 1750 when it sold the last of its properties to a local trader. The Hanseatic warehouse, for years nearly derelict, has recently been restored and functions again as an administrative headquarters, though now for the local authority.

The river gives: it provided the access to the Midlands that created much of King's Lynn's wealth. But the river also takes away, and all along King Street one sees solid boards slotted before the street doors as protection against the mud produced by flooding. St Margaret's Church bears a frightening indication of the power of the river, showing the flood level during the Great Storm of 1741 which destroyed much of the church.

Following the curious duality of its nature, King's Lynn has two guildhalls. The Guildhall of the Holy Trinity in Saturday Market is still the town's centre of government, proudly displaying its rich regalia in a specially designed museum in the crypt. Along King Street is St George's Hall, all but derelict until saved by 'the inspiration and generosity' of a local worthy. It now belongs to the National Trust and, as the Fermoy Centre, is the home of the successful King's Lynn festival. The hall is a model of modern restoration for while the historic building has been saved (and the splendid hammer-beam roof alone would have made restoration worthwhile), it also discharges a social function as a restaurant and picture gallery, the gardens extending right down to the Ouse. Considering how little English towns use their rivers, the way in which modern Lynn incorporates its sullen, unlovely river into daily life is remarkable.

One of the town's gates still defies the demands of traffic and in The Walks it is possible to trace the line of the town's walls. King's Lynn has, unhappily, allowed itself to be afflicted by the suburban sprawl of our century, but the nucleus of this splendid trading centre is still clearly identifiable and sound.

The Customs House, built in 1683, reflects the town's past prosperity as a sea port.

LOUTH, LINCOLNSHIRE

'Loud river' *Anglo-Saxon*
Population 13,296 *Market :* Friday, Saturday *Cattle :* Wednesday

THE Lincolnshire Wolds rise suddenly out of the fenland like the broaching of a great green whale. The total flatness of Lincolnshire is exhilarating, unlike the timid undulations of neighbouring Norfolk and Nottinghamshire, but the Wolds do come as a refreshing contrast. Travelling from Lincoln in the west, the spire of Louth Church is seen long before the town is visible, rising up from its rich foothills, the whole bearing a remarkable resemblance to a nineteenth-century steel engraving. Nor is the traveller disappointed on coming closer, for the road swings on down past large Victorian houses, each in its ample garden until, abruptly, it becomes the Georgian street called Westgate, the setting for the immense crocketed spire that has beckoned the traveller onward for the last 10 miles.

The Wolds are barely 500 feet high at their topmost point, and extend north and south for only about 20 miles with a width of perhaps 4 or 5 miles. But they mark off a different kind of country with Louth the undoubted capital of a tiny kingdom of villages and small towns set in the narrow strip between Wolds and sea. Although the town appears in the Domesday Book, testifying to its economic importance, its origin is unknown and it enters history, like so many other English towns, as a protégé of the local monastery. A colony of monks from Fountains Abbey built one of the largest Cistercian houses about a mile east of the present town. Destruction after the Dissolution was total: the ditch called Monks' Dike (a conduit to supply the ponds and moats) and a few fragments above ground are all that remain. The monks seem to have established themselves genuinely among the locals for the people of Louth took a major part in the Lincolnshire Rising of 1536. Henry VIII was enraged, describing them as 'the rude commons of one of the most brute and beastly shires of the whole realm'. He hanged a number of the townsfolk in their own market place and took the vicar off for more detailed treatment at Tyburn.

The church is undoubtedly Louth's glory, as splendid close-up as it is from a distance. It is mostly a fifteenth-century building, completed within two or three decades by 1441. Tower and crowning spire are almost exactly equal in height which gives it that dual effect of being at once commanding and graceful. The stone carvings around the walls, though not as prodigal or as fine as at Wells, give a delightfully lively picture of contemporary events and people. There is some good modern work too, both in stone and wood: the roof, in particular, is an unusually sensitive Victorian rendering of local style.

The buildings in and around the market place are 'provincial' in the best possible sense of that term – that is, they have not as yet succumbed to the bland uniformity of similar municipalities. Doubtless one or two of the ironmongers' shops and general stores would deeply upset a time-and-motion expert and his actuarial colleague, but they continue to make a living for their owners. For most of the shops are still owner-occupied, the dead hand of the multiple store as yet not too evident.

Dominating the market place is the insouciant Market Hall, built in 1867 in a style called 'Byzantine Gothic' but establishing its own quirky presence. It is functional too, providing a covered market for a wide variety of stalls. The nineteenth century has undoubtedly left its mark in Louth, for the Town Hall is another product of the period, built thirteen years before the Market Hall and embellished with rich interior decoration. In the Council Chamber is an excellent painting by a local

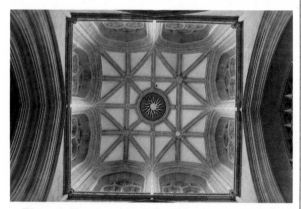

The magnificent vaulting below the west tower in Louth Church. The hexagonal spire, completed in 1515, is a landmark visible from miles away.

Market day in Louth. It was a bookseller in this market place who published Tennyson's first work. The poet was educated at Louth Grammar School.

artist, William Brown, which depicts a birds-eye view of the town seen from the church tower. Painted in 1850, it is an expression of local pride that one expects to find in an Italian, rather than an English town. The grammar school, though established late in the thirteenth century, did not receive its royal charter from Edward VI until 1551. In common with many similar schools in the country it was endowed with some of the loot acquired through the dissolution of the monasteries. Physically, it did not survive the building urge of the Victorians, being rebuilt in 1869, though it still plays an educational role in the town as part of a girls' school.

MALDON, ESSEX

'Hill with a cross' *Anglo-Saxon*
Population : 15,250 *Market :* Thursday, Saturday

HERE, in the very heart of subtopia where the suburbs of London all but touch the commuter towns of Essex and both are fringed with a dispirited belt of seaside towns, occurred one of the great battles of English history. Like so many proudly remembered English battles it is a famous defeat, echoing down through history in two poignant lines of Saxon poetry, taken from *The Battle of Maldon*:

> Thought shall be the harder, heart the keener
> Mood shall be the more as our might lessons.

If you stand on the roof of Maldon's fifteenth century Moot Hall you can see, just outside the town on the misty salt marshes, the place where the Battle of Maldon took place in AD 991. The town must have been big enough by then to be worth plundering for a Viking fleet had painstakingly navigated its way up the Blackwater river. Brithnoth, ealderman of Essex, placed a shieldwall between the invading murderers and the town but the Saxons went down almost to a man, providing the subject for one of the great Saxon epics. Presumably, the Vikings would then have treated the town to the usual pattern of

destruction, but its founders had chosen its site too well for it to be totally obliterated by the most dedicated marauder.

The town stands on a high hill above the flood plain. A main street, later known as Market Street, descends steeply to a complete maritime harbour, although the town is some 14 miles from the sea. Here, the smaller River Chelm joins the larger Blackwater, making an ideal river road to the high seas.

The Romans built a port at Heybridge, half a mile outside the town. It was never developed into a major town, probably because the Romans were already thoroughly well established at Colchester some 10 miles away. But the Maldon locality provided a substance which, if not quite worth its weight in gold, was frequently used in lieu of it. Salt – so vital a substance that Roman soldiers received part of their salary in it. At the time of Domesday in 1086 there were no fewer than forty-five salt pans, four belonging to the king. Salt was as important a source of government revenue as tobacco is today and was treated accordingly : at the time of Trafalgar

The Heybridge Basin at Maldon, still a thriving port 2000 years after the Romans established it.

Boats on the Hythe, the name given to the main quay at Maldon, with the parish church behind. In the right background can be seen examples of the great Thames barges.

tax on it had risen to £30 a ton. Then Cheshire-mined rock salt undercut prices and the Maldon salt industry collapsed. One firm, established in 1777, survived and is flourishing today, the modern fashion for 'natural foods' boosting its prosperity. Production technique has changed little since the Romans introduced it, and to the uninitiated there seems no relationship between the decidedly unap-petizing water of the creek from which the factory draws its raw material, and the dazzling mounds of sea-salt that emerge.

The sea, both as highway and as salt-producer, has therefore been Maldon's livelihood for centuries. Henry II granted it a charter in 1171, making it one of the very earliest of English charter boroughs and in return the burgesses had to provide one ship for the navy for forty days when called upon to do so. To the visitor, the town presents two entirely different attractions: the purely urban centre, mostly Georgian, and the maritime area. The Heybridge Basin, site of the original Roman port, is virtually a textbook model of late eighteenth- and early nineteenth-century canal en-gineering, for here the Chelmer, the Blackwater and the main Navigation canals all meet. Immediately below the town is the Hythe or quay, the true maritime centre of the town. The Maldon Society has produced an excellent Maritime Trail, extend-ing for the remarkable length of some 12 miles.

It is from the Hythe that the great Thames barges used to operate, and where many of them were built, among them the *Record Reign*, 'the loveliest barge ever built' according to Hervey Benham, historian of the East Coast barges. These large craft with their shallow draught and immense spritsail rigs seem almost impossibly clumsy in confined waterways. But their appearance was a process of evolution rather than design, and perfectly suited their envir-onment, dominating transport along the East Coast until the modern development of roads. They almost died out, but have a renewed life now as pleasure boats and the Hythe is again crowded with these craft and their great ochre sails.

Maldon lost its railway station in the 1960s, and though this has probably saved it from becoming a purely commuter town, it is at the price of being battered by traffic using Market Hill as a main artery. The outstanding building in the High Street is the Moot Hall, with its elegant colonnaded façade. But its interior is, if anything, even more interesting with the heavily timbered council room on the first floor and, above all, the unusual – and probably unique – 'newell' brick staircase which may well be contemporary with the building.

SAFFRON WALDEN, ESSEX

'Valley where saffron grew' Anglo-Saxon
Population : 12,515 Market : Tuesday, Saturday

ESSEX is a curiously mixed county. Of all those adjacent to London it has been the most maltreated by town planners, with ribbon development and the dreariest of light industries stretching far into the so-called countryside. But, amongst the un-distinguished 'Mon Reposes' and 'Dunromins' of the suburban belt are any number of fascinating vernacular houses, combining a remarkably wide range of materials – timber, thatch, brick, flint and above all, plaster. And among the brash 'new towns' are true towns which seem to have made only the most cursory concessions to the twentieth century, stubbornly – and happily – maintaining their ancient identities.

Saffron Walden is pre-eminently one such, a fact most evident in the street pattern surrounding the market place. Here is a classic example of market-place encroachment for these narrow streets, lined with low, oddly chunky buildings, are quite obviously the permanent form of the rows of market stalls that would have been first set up when the town was granted its market charter in 1295. Some of them still bear the name of the dominant trade – Butcher Road, Tanners' Way, Mercers' Row, Drapers' Row – and together, they form perhaps the clearest surviving example of the pattern of a medieval market place.

Human occupation goes back a long way in East

The mysterious maze on the outskirts of the town. It plays a part in many children's games today, but originally it probably had a ritual significance.

Anglia. Long before the coming of the Romans, early settlers, hacking a community out of the thick woodlands on the slopes by the River Cam, threw up a series of defensive earthworks near the future town. The Saxons put up a wooden church and castle forming the nucleus of the present town and the Normans, in their usual way, turned wooden castle into massive stone fort. They also built the first stone church on the site of the old Saxon church. But, in the unpredictable way of history, the castle virtually melted away (all that remains is the core of some of the walls, looking oddly like a natural stone outcrop) and the church itself is an entirely 'English' building for it was mostly rebuilt in the late fifteenth century. Even in a hilly country, this superb church would be impressive: in the flat Essex countryside it dominates effortlessly but still maintains an intimate relationship with the town, its green surroundings seeming to merge into the neighbouring streets.

Saffron Walden has been fortunate in its industries, for as one died off another rose to replace it, bringing in sufficient wealth to build the merchants' solid houses, but not overwhelming the town with vast factories. As with most English towns, wool was its first staple trade, but when this went into a relative decline the trade in saffron was there to fill the gap. The saffron crocus, with its distinctive purple flower, spread its great carpets in the locality for nearly 200 years during the sixteenth and seventeenth centuries. The plant has four quite separate commercial uses – as dye, as condiment, as medicine, and as perfume. Dyeing was its most important commercial usage and when this came to an end in the eighteenth century, the town took up malting.

Meanwhile it had developed as a market centre. Like most East Anglian townships, it created a central space for its market, instead of using the High Street as is more common in the south of England. The result is a compact town centre with the High Street forming the western boundary, church and castle together forming the northern boundary and common land to the east. On this common, incidentally, is the mysterious maze cut

Saffron Walden's market place, surrounded by the surviving traces of medieval merchants' 'rows'.

The art of pargeting, so very characteristic of Essex and Suffolk, is seen at its best in the range of buildings once known as the Sun Inn.

into the turf. Its origin is unknown, though it is almost certainly prehistoric and of ritual significance: the first documented reference to it is in 1699 when its shape was recut. An elaborate courtship game was played on it in the nineteenth century, with swains attempting to find their way to a girl at the centre, and even today it provides considerable entertainment for children and visitors.

The chief attractions of Saffron Walden are its inns and its solid burgers' houses. On the High Street is the great Saffron Hotel, a sixteenth-century coaching inn appropriately named and coloured, while on the corner of the High Street is the timbered Cross Keys, its low, dark rooms very snug on a winter's day. Both private and public buildings display pargeting, that highly decorative device achieved by moulding plaster and seen at its best in Essex. Outstanding even in Saffron Walden is the former Sun Inn – an immense, rambling building. Pargeting covers it completely, but the major feature is an illustration of a local legend, that of Thomas Hickathrift and the giant. Executed in the seventeenth-century the life-size figures, though crudely modelled, are full of energy.

SPALDING, LINCOLNSHIRE

'Land of the Spalde tribe' *Anglo-Saxon*
Population: 18,223 *Market:* Tuesday, Saturday *Cattle:* Tuesday *Pigs:* Friday

FROM about the first week in May until the end of August, in a large green field known as the 'Arena' on the outskirts of Spalding, there is a circle of immense figures – mythological, symbolical, satirical – looking rather like the figures on an old-fashioned roundabout. At the beginning of the period they are brilliantly coloured, for each is made up of thousands of tulip heads pinned onto straw, which is itself tied to a metal frame. At the end of the summer, when the heads have fallen off, the straw base is put to the torch in one tremendous bonfire and the frames are taken away to be refashioned into the floats for the next year's Spalding Flower Parade.

The extraordinary thing about the parade is that it is an entirely spontaneous development. Only too often, 'traditional' parades and festivals are musty, self-conscious revivals of defunct customs or beady-eyed advertizing gimmicks. The parade is born of the locality for the beautiful blooms that bring it to life are, in effect, the waste products of the bulb industry. It is the bulbs themselves which are harvested while the blooms, picked with the absolute minimum of stem, have no commercial value. Twenty-six years ago the locals decided to use the discarded flower heads in a domestic festival: currently, some 300,000 people pour into the town on a Saturday in early May to watch the parade. There is a core of commercial involvement, for each of the floats costs its sponsor between £2000 and £5000, but the labour required to pin in, by hand, hundreds of thousands of separate blooms could be achieved only by enthusiastic volunteers.

During the four or five hours that this, the very youngest of English festivals lasts, the parade passes by what is, apart from the Ashmolean Museum in Oxford, the oldest museum in Britain. The Gentlemen's Society was founded in 1709 by a local barrister and antiquary, Maurice Johnson, who, through his connections in London was on personal terms with some of the leading scientists, intellectuals and poets of the day. Isaac Newton, Alexander Pope, John Gay, George Vertue, Sir Hans Sloane (whose library was to become the nucleus of the British Museum) – all were members of this extra-

Ayscoughfee Hall. This fifteenth-century manor house was the home of Maurice Johnson, founder of the Gentlemen's Society.

ordinary society in a small Lincolnshire town in the eighteenth century. More joined during the nineteenth and twentieth centuries: Tennyson, Lord Curzon, Giles Gilbert Scott, each contributing something whether it was personal expertise, some literally priceless gift or an amusing object either found, acquired or inherited. The little museum in Broad Street became the society's first permanent home in 1911. Before that, it met in the home of one or other of its members and its slowly expanding collection of rarities and curiosities was also moved from one place to another. Today, this gentlemen's 'cabinet of curiosities' houses a Caxton book that rubs shoulders with Chinese ceramics, local paintings of only local value side by side with a rare Flemish tapestry, Sir Christopher Hatton's astrolabe alongside a vile, blood-stained spike designed to keep a Victorian child's head upright. All this, not to mention a priceless library of local history which would grace many a metropolis, in a small market town.

Most English towns turn away from their river, or entomb it in brick. The River Welland is the dominant feature of Spalding, running confidently through it, edged with green turf, as though it were a

One of the extraordinary, colourful tableaux made for the Spalding Festival. It consists of thousands of tulip heads, each attached by hand to a base of straw.

main road, which, to some extent it was at one period. The town began life as an adjunct to a great priory and a castle; both have utterly disappeared, apart from street names and an enigmatic structure known as the Prior's Oven. From the sixteenth century onwards Spalding earned its living as a trading centre, bringing in corn and coleseed, sending out coal and timber – humdrum enough activities which nevertheless brought in a comfortable income for its citizens. The town's principal private house, Ayscoughfee Hall, was once the home of Maurice Johnson. Basically a fifteenth century manor house, it is currently undergoing much needed restoration after which the ground floor will house a tourist information centre and museum. Most of the surviving houses in the town centre and, particularly, along the river banks are decent, solid eighteenth- and early nineteenth-century town houses. Spalding, indeed, is a perfect example of the slow spread of architectural styles for

Lying close to the River Welland is another of Spalding's inns, the White Horse, its painted brick and thatched roof dating from the early seventeenth century.

The little River Welland almost acts as a watery High Street for Spalding, for it is lined on both sides with handsome town houses.

the houses whose fashion was established in London in the late eighteenth century were here built mostly from the 1820s onwards.

The market place is tucked away from the river, its main building the fine White Hart inn whose eighteenth-century front graces a much older building with the typical yard of the coaching inn. Upstairs, one is shown with pride the room used by Mary, Queen of Scots, which makes a change from the rooms used by her cousin and great adversary. A new civic centre, forbidding in appearance but with a certain impressive strength, looms over the square. The church is unusually distant from the market place, away on the other side of the river; at one time it was within the boundaries of the priory, but the prior, disliking this close proximity to his flock, moved the parish church to its present position. It spans some six centuries, from the thirteenth to the nineteenth and, despite the attention of seventeenth-century iconoclasts and nineteenth-century restorers, the church maintains both presence and character.

STAMFORD, LINCOLNSHIRE

'Stone ford' *Anglo-Saxon*
Population: 16,153 *Market:* Friday, Saturday *Cattle:* Monday

THIS quintessentially English town shares, with Oxford and Bath, an oddly Italianate quality. It is most evident from an aerial photograph in which the town appears as one vast sculptured building with only here and there that greenery usually associated with English towns. The reason is, probably, because it is built of one material – stone – and because it lacks suburban sprawl. The approach from the south is one of the most satisfying of all urban experiences. The country stops and the town begins. But it is not any town. Framing the vista is the splendidly arrogant sign of the George Inn; beyond it, the stone-built street becomes a stone-built bridge and again a stone-built street, sweeping up in an act of obeisance to the splendour of St Mary's Church. And that is merely the foyer or entrance hall, as it were. Beyond St Mary's the town divides into two, like the wings of a great palace: on the left is the Sheep Market and Red Lion Square, on the right, the High Street.

In 1967 Stamford became the first town in England to be recognized as a conservation area under the Civic Administration Act. In effect, the entire town was thereby legally regarded as a work of art, its multitude of details blending to form a unified whole. The architectural richness of the town can be estimated from the fact that, within an area some 1000 yards by 400 yards, are concentrated

The compact nature of this stone town is well brought out in an aerial view. St Mary's Church can be seen at the centre and St John's with Sheep Market is on the left.

The elaborate tomb of one of the Cecils – the local 'great family' – in St Martin's Church, Stamford.

economic. In 1461 a Lancastrian army burnt the town to the ground, five churches alone surviving. Then the wool trade, the town's staple industry, declined disastrously and finally, by the mid sixteenth century the Welland silted up and ceased to be navigable. By the early seventeenth century what had been a bustling, thriving town was apparently dying, its population having dwindled to some 1500.

But its pulse was still strong enough to be revived and the event which brought that about was the construction of the Welland Navigation canal.

The Burghley almshouses were established by Benedictine monks but were later considerably enlarged by Lord Burghley.

half the listed buildings of the entire county. And its history is as rich as its architecture, not so much because events of national importance happened here (though there are plenty of these) but because it possessed, or was affected by most of the elements that constitute English towns.

Stamford, established in the very heart of Roman Britain, owed its birth to the fact that Saxons strongly disliked living in Roman towns. There was a military settlement at Great Casterton a mile or so away, and doubtless the Romans would have had a form of stronghold at this 'stone ford', the only place where the River Welland could be crossed on foot. But there was nothing permanent here and the Saxons had a clean slate upon which to work. Their town was in the front line of battle between Danes and Saxons and in due course was ceded to the savage, but energetic newcomers and became one of the five Danelaw burhs. It prospered, as did all Danish towns: it even had a university in the early fourteenth century, though Oxford and Cambridge promptly combined to throttle it. Then two catastrophes struck, the one military, the other

Though less than 10 miles long, this canal possessed twelve locks, and through it the town's livelihood was renewed. Most of the new industry was agricultural – tanning of hides, malting, hemp-weaving – and markets grew up for the sale of general produce and cattle: the Sheep Market is a relic of this period. And this new source of wealth created the attractive face of Stamford that we see today. Architecturally, the destruction of 1461 can be construed as a benefit if the present town can be regarded as the long-term result.

The beautiful local stone is a limestone, relatively easy to work. (Unfortunately, it tends to absorb dirt and grime quickly though this can be readily

Celebrated for its architecture, Stamford boasts six notable churches as well as the remains of a Benedictine priory and a Carmelite monastery.

removed.) Unlike those of Ludlow, the houses were not the homes of county gentry but solid local citizens, contemptuous of gewgaws and frills. Individually, the houses are plain, ornamentation for the most part appearing in the form of architraves and a dramatic flaring of keystones over windows. The great George Inn is another excellent example of eighteenth-century refacing. Apart from that great signboard, one could pass the building by without another glance, so well does it fit into the Georgian street. But on entering that modest doorway, one is aware of another world where room upon room clusters round a superb courtyard. Today, as heavy lorries pound our towns to pieces, and pedestrians play Russian roulette with endless private cars, it is easy to forget that road traffic once brought wealth. Stamford straddles the Great North Road and this superb inn is only one of many whose wealth was made by through traffic: in the early nineteenth century some seventy stage or mail coaches passed through the town.

Although it is Stamford's homogeneity that impresses the visitor, there are any number of architecturally outstanding buildings. Nearby is the enormous mass of Burghley Park, built by Elizabeth I's counsellor, William Cecil, and still inhabited by his descendants (see *Great English Houses* in this series). It is the existence of the great park, coming right up to the town, that has preserved that marvellous entry from the south. The Town Hall, built as late as 1776, emphasizes in its architecture that Italianate style which is so noticeable from the air. Two splendid churches, St Martin's and St Mary's, punctuate each end of the river crossing (Cecil is buried in a remarkable ornate tomb in St Martin's). Browne's Hospital on Broad Street is an almshouse which, built by a wealthy merchant in the fifteenth century, enlarged in the nineteenth and 'modernized' in the 1960s, somehow still retains its ancient imprint. Tucked away up a flight of steps, it forms a tiny oasis of green amidst the universal stone. In the 1970s a Georgian theatre that had degenerated into a public hall used for jumble sales was restored as part of the Stamford Arts Centre.

THAXTED, ESSEX

'Place where thatch was gathered' *Anglo-Saxon*
Population: 2000 *Market*: suspended

THAXTED has all but fallen victim to its own beauty, and its proximity to large and unattractive conurbations. As a result, the town has more than its share of antique and gift shops, and there is an undoubted self-consciousness about its restaurants and inns. But the town is solidly rooted, returning to its own life style outside the tourist seasons. And, as a bonus, its beauty has created a strongly active civic society. The heir to two lively predecessors, the present Thaxted Society was largely responsible for the promotion of a comprehensive architectural and historical survey of the town.

Thaxted falls into two natural halves. Crowning the hill is the great parish church with its attendant green and almshouses, offset incongruously but dramatically by an immense windmill built in 1804. At the bottom of the hill is the 600-year-old Guildhall, regnant over its own little kingdom. Connecting the two halves is an ancient street, now a footpath known as Stony Lane, and the main road, a splendid swooping curve of Watling Street.

Even in East Anglia, noted for its great cathedral-like parish churches, Thaxted Church is outstanding. Within, it has the great height, flooded with cool light from lofty windows, that one comes to associate with churches in this part of the country. It is virtually impossible to summarize its architectural details according to any school or period for its building extended over nearly 200 years, longer than the time required to build many a cathedral. Work began on the site of an earlier church in 1340 and was brought to a conclusion when roof and clerestory were completed in 1510. The project was initiated in a combined operation by the local lord of the manor, the townsfolk and, in particular, the Cutlers' Company. There is no obvious reason why this small East Anglian township should have produced a band of men skilled in making and sharpening knives and swords when their neighbours were finding a living in producing wool or saffron. But certainly the early affluence of the town was founded on this industry.

Indeed, so wealthy and powerful had the cutlers become that, in 1390, while the church was still 130 years from completion, they set out to build their own Guildhall. It is a sturdy timber building, its three storeys jettying out to give a low-browed, beetling expression to the building. It rests upon vast oak pillars, the ground floor being open to form a market house. The first floor was probably originally an open gallery while the upper floor housed the hall of the guild and living quarters for the warden.

The cutlery industry began to decline in the mid sixteenth century and, the town being raised to borough status with concomitant privileges of Mayor and Corporation, the Guildhall was taken over as Thaxted's administrative headquarters. The building survived the attention of the Georgians who restored it in 1714. Only too often, current taste demanded the covering up of all naked timbers with decorous brick but the restorers of the Guildhall contented themselves mostly with enclosing the first floor, altering the roof and introducing pargeting. The building was then used as a grammar school until 1878 and another restoration of 1911 left the building looking much as it would have done in the Middle Ages.

Thaxted's windmill last turned in 1907. It became derelict during the 1950s but has now been restored to full working order and is managed by a Trust.

Thaxted's almshouses. The thatched building on the left, behind the flowering cherry tree, was originally a priest's house. Those on the right were custom-built in 1714.

The open ground floor of the Guildhall discharged the traditional function of the covered market, whilst the surrounding area would have acted as the market place. The market in Thaxted, however, has had varying fortunes. The decline of the cutlery industry brought about the simultaneous decline of the market but, with the revival of agriculture in the early nineteenth century it, too, came back to life. Currently, it is again in the doldrums, probably because of the proximity of Saffron Walden, now easily reached by road transport, and its future revival is a matter of debate.

The lower town of Thaxted, endowed with some fine buildings, has a brisk, sleeves-rolled-up, workaday look about it. By walking up Stony Lane and through the churchyard, one enters into quite a different ambience. In the churchyard itself two long, single-storeyed structures form a frame for the distant windmill. The thatched building, still known as The Chantry, was a priest's house until 1589 when it was converted into an almshouse. Its parallel neighbour was custom-built as an almshouse in 1714 and still provides shelter for elderly people, though now for only three couples instead of

the sixteen individuals for whom it was originally intended. The windmill beyond was built by a local farmer, John Webb, on the site of an earlier mill and is therefore the last survivor of at least three working mills in the town. Webb's mill last worked in 1907 and, after a brief period as a youth centre in the 1930s, had become derelict by the 1950s. In 1970 a Trust was formed to restore it and, complete with enormous sails, it now functions as a rural museum.

The closing of the Thaxted Light Railway in 1953 has rather isolated the town, for it is on a secondary road. Apart from tourists, people tend to pass through the town on their way to or from Saffron Walden or Great Dunmow and its changed circumstances are reflected in its declining population figures – from 2527 in 1848 to around 2000 today. But towns are no longer economically dependent upon indigenous populations and Thaxted has, aesthetically, gained from the decline, being spared to a large extent twentieth-century suburban expansion. It is possible to stand on the great shoulder of the town beneath John Webb's windmill, looking out into open country and yet, by turning round, gain the town centre in two minutes' brisk walk.

The town naturally falls into two halves, the church crowning the hill and the Guildhall dominating the market.

WYMONDHAM. NORFOLK

'Estate of Wigmund's people' Anglo-Saxon
Population: 9811 Market: Friday

THE twentieth-century bypass saved this town and, incidentally, corrected an injustice which had been committed 800 years before. The first prior of the great abbey, William the Conqueror's ex-retainer William d'Albini, had declared that the noise of traffic passing the abbey disturbed his monks at prayer. And, being who he was, William d'Albini was able to divert traffic through the town. The modern bypass means that the uninformed traveller can sweep past Wymondham, scarcely aware of its presence. But it also means that the townsfolk can again possess their town in relative peace after half a century of siege by road transport.

Despite the superb double towers of the abbey ruins, the ancient street names of the town declare, unequivocally, that it was a place of small craftsmen and traders. Bellrope Lane, Brewery Lane, Chandler's Hill are all self-evident names; less obvious are Rattle Row (so called from the continual noise of the looms which created much of the town's prosperity); Spooner Row (from the manufacture of wooden spoons), and Fairland Street, the area where fairs used to be held. Not far away, along the road to Norwich, is an ancient pump, used to water the livestock bought at Wymondham's cattle market and destined for the great metropolis 10 miles away. And near that pump are the squat remains of an

Norfolk towns vie with each other over their town signs based on trades or historical associations. Wymondham's shows weaving, spoon-making and the abbey.

ancient oak tree – Kett's Oak – marking the gathering place of the tragic local peasant's revolt of 1549. Wymondham, in other words, is most firmly linked to its agricultural background.

Two buildings dominate the town, illustrating its social polarization: the magnificent Abbey Church, begun in 1107, and the two-storeyed, timbered Market Cross, built between 1617 and 1618 on the site of a much older cross. The extraordinary contrasting towers of the church reflect the 'town-gown' tension which was so frequently a characteristic of towns hosting major ecclesiastical foundations. The church was originally supposed to be shared between monks and townsfolk, but so bitter were the quarrels between them, so endless the rows regarding who owned what of the church that the

The dramatically differing towers of Wymondham Abbey are evidence of the battle between townsfolk and clergy in the fifteenth century as to who owned which part.

pope was obliged to intervene, dividing the building between them. Even that did not stop the quarrels and in the fifteenth century (over two centuries after the pope's adjudication) each party built its own belfry. Little of the abbey itself survives, apart from the gatehouse and a superb nave, its Norman arches and triforium surmounted by a fifteenth-century roof of great delicacy. Yet the church found a new lease of life after the Dissolution as Wymondham's parish church.

The town's market rights were granted in 1440 and were revived only in the present century. But a market cross stood on Market Hill from at least the late thirteenth century until it was destroyed accidentally by fire in 1615. The present cross, built at a cost of £25 7s od, rapidly became the very heart of the market and, hence, of the town. The market court assembled in the octagonal upper room every Tuesday to try offences against the market laws. Dues were paid here, and licenses inspected. In the open space below, beggars plied their trade, labourers and servants assembled for their annual hiring and banns of marriage were published from the steps. It has a simple but sturdy dignity, built of local oak and carved with the emblems of the wood turnery which was one of the town's staple trades.

Fire, that scourge of medieval towns, razed the place in 1615 and the face that Wymondham presents is therefore largely seventeenth-century. But it still possesses one of the many 'oldest inns' in England, the splendidly named Green Dragon. Although it comes fairly low in this league, the inn's foundation is undoubtedly late fourteenth-century and it has happily escaped the brewers' passion for gutting and 'modernizing', presenting to the visitor that multiplicity of small rooms, each with its specialized function and unique characteristics that are part of the charm of country pubs. Becket's Chapel, too, escaped the fire. It was probably part of the Guild of St Thomas the Martyr, one of the most popular of medieval saints, and was built in 1175. Somehow it survived both the Dissolution and the seventeenth-century iconoclasts, although used for a number of humdrum purposes, including brief spells as a coal house, a lock-up and a fire station. Currently it is being used for a purpose more in keeping with its original role, for it is now the local branch of the County Library.

Although entirely modern in appearance, the market at Wymondham is still centred round the seventeenth-century market 'cross', in fact a substantial building.

THE NORTH

BARNARD CASTLE, CO. DURHAM

'Castle of Bernard (Baliol)' *French*
Population: 5016 *Market:* Wednesday

THIS is another of England's towns that was brought into existence to supply the needs of a castle, instead of the castle being built to hold or protect the town. A Frenchman called Guy de Baliol, lord of Bailleu in Picardy, began the process some time before 1100 when he raised an immense mound by cutting a ditch through a massive rock which rose above the River Tees. It was a natural place for a castle, just at the end of the Stainmore gap across the Pennines, and about half a century later Guy's great-nephew, Bernard, rebuilt the existing wooden castle in stone. His name was thereafter associated with it and in due course became the name of the little town which developed at its feet. By 1178 the community had evidently acquired an identity separate from the castle for Bernard, in his capacity of lord of the manor, granted it a charter in that year.

In recent years, the regrettable municipal tendency to demolish 'slums' instead of renovating

The building that created, and gave its name to the town of Barnard Castle. Although not immediately evident from this viewpoint, the castle is totally ruinous.

The first permanent houses of the town appeared along this steep street, known as the Bank, which is crowned by the distinctive market cross.

them where appropriate has cost Barnard Castle many of its older buildings. It is, however, still possible to trace the probable sequence of the town's development. The first houses would have appeared on the flat ground by the river and then, as the town expanded, buildings gradually encroached upon the steep hill now known as the Bank. The fine market place, which is, in effect, a continuation of the Bank, though separated from it by the Market Cross, clearly shows the sequence which must have taken place in all similar towns. The castellan would have looked with a cold eye on houses appearing against the castle wall itself, thus providing shelter for possible attackers, so the first houses here, in the true heart of the town, appeared on the far side of the market place. It was only when the castle began to fall into ruin in the seventeenth century that houses crept along its base, on the left-hand side of the market place. In some of them, particularly the inns, it is still possible to detect the line of the castle ditch for the stone-flagged entry passages run slightly downwards.

Bernard Baliol's charter was a generous one, launching the town into history with some valuable privileges and possessions. Curiously, he conceded the prestigious (and valuable) gallows right to the burghers. Galgate, a street as delightful as the market place and running at right angles to it, is a reminder of this right which usually entitled the hangman to the victim's effects. With the building of the bridge across the Tees, the town would have become the metropolis for a locality of small hamlets and scattered farms that is still wild even today. The last military action in which the castle figured took place during the Rising of the North in 1569, when it was besieged for eleven days by the Catholic rebels before surrendering. Thereafter, though by now a royal castle, its effective life was at an end and Barnard Castle entered its role as a small, but prosperous market town. Its local industries – tanning, weaving, harness-making – provided a comfortable income (reflected, in particular, by a number of well-designed Georgian houses), but it escaped the physical blight of the Industrial Revolution. The nineteenth century saw a flood of gimcrack housing, but the stone-built core of the town survived.

The Market Cross or Hall is very much the badge

The eighteenth-century market cross of Barnard Castle functioned as a covered market, lock-up and, in the upper storey, as council chamber.

of the town. Its survival is remarkable for it is at the junction of three main streets and after its function had ceased, there must have been strong and continuous pressure to demolish it in order to improve traffic flow. Happily, such pressure was resisted and the town retains a superb eighteenth-century building that reflects its peak of prosperity. It is octagonal in shape, with an elegant lantern which once served as the town's record office. Immediately below, and supporting it, are strong piers enclosed to form a gaol. The whole is surrounded by an arcade or verandah, supported by simple Doric pillars which vary in height to take account of

the steep slope. Just distinguishable in the weather vane are two small holes, made by bullets. In 1804 rival marksmen fired from the doorway of the Turk's Head, a hundred yards away. They seem to have been equally matched.

On the outskirts of Barnard Castle is a building one would expect to find in Paris or London rather than in a small north country town. This is the palatial Bowes Museum, built in French Renaissance style in 1869 by John Bowes, son of the 10th earl of Strathmore, to house his collection of art. It was first opened to the public, while remaining a private museum, in 1892.

DURHAM, CO. DURHAM

'Island with a hill' *Anglo-Saxon*
Population : 26,242 *Market :* Saturday

A PRINCE-BISHOP's seat of state that one can walk across in five minutes; a medieval jewel in a once industrial setting; a place where pilgrims and miners rub shoulders with each other (and are frequently the same people); the home of England's third oldest university, and a vital link in the trades union system – Durham is all these simultaneously. And even if the city had no particular history or noteworthy buildings, its site would still confer an unforgettable and imperishable presence for it stands high on a sandstone bluff with the River Wear coiling around it like a living moat.

The site of the city reflects its original function – a frontier bastion against the raiding Scots. But it owes its foundation to a saint, or rather to that saint's devoted disciples who believed, with some justification, that they were taking part in a miracle. Cuthbert had died on the holy island of Lindisfarne in 687. A century later in 995, his still uncorrupted body began its extraordinary wanderings as the monks responsible for its safety fled first to the mainland from a Danish raiding party and then, for the next century, moved from one temporary resting place to another, pursued by various enemies. It was not until 1070 that he was brought to rest, finally, in Durham, only to be disturbed again a

The Gallilee Chapel of Durham Cathedral, enclosing the shrine of St Cuthbert in whose honour the cathedral was founded.

The market place, Durham, with its statue of Charles Vane-Stewart, 3rd marquess of Londonderry, as Lord Lieutenant of the county.

generation later when, in 1104, he was placed in a splendid shrine in the new cathedral. There he remained until 1542 when Henry VIII's hatchet men broke up the shrine, stole its treasures, and discovered the saint's body still uncorrupt. It was buried on the same spot as the shrine but was disturbed yet again in 1827, by which time it had become a skeleton, and – incredibly – once more in 1899 for anatomical investigation. It is now sealed, permanently, one hopes. But it is still an object of veneration and pilgrimage, although the twelfth-century bronze sanctuary knocker, placed on the north door in accordance with his wishes, has recently been replaced by a replica.

Durham was a lively centre of resistance against the Normans, murdering at least one bishop imposed by the Conqueror. And though William took savage reprisals it was not until his son and successor, William Rufus, decided to combine bishopric with earldom that the city was finally brought into the Norman fold. It was a dangerous step for the prince-bishop was, almost literally, a king within his own domain, laying down his own laws, coining his own money, raising his own army. But the experiment worked until the Reformation when, in 1541, the cathedral was refounded as a secular (i.e. non-monastic) foundation – stripped of much of its power but still a cathedral. The great building still reflects the power of its bishops. In England, only Salisbury can compare with it in the speed of its erection for, begun in 1093 it was completed forty years later. As such, it is the most complete, most homogenous Norman church in England. Even the brutal 'restoration' of the late eighteenth century, when a thousand tons of stone were shaved off the building, could not impair its dignity.

A bow-shot from the cathedral is the castle, the home of these singularly unspiritual ghostly fathers. It is a classic Norman castle raised on its symmetrical green mound, strong enough to resist the Scots, elegant enough to provide a very comfortable life style for its occupants. It functions still, though now as one of the colleges of the University, and some idea of its spendour can be gained from the Great Hall. One of the biggest medieval chambers in England – rivalled only by London's Westminster Hall – it is today the college dining room, open to visitors out of term.

The castle closes off the neck of land that joins the escarpment to the mainland. In effect, castle and cathedral between them occupy what was the

Castle and cathedral together crown the sandstone bluff high above the River Weare, making a formidable fortress. The river, curving round at its base, almost creates an island.

original extent of the city, the only secular and private buildings belonging to those associated with these two giant establishments. The heart could have become fossilized were it not for the fact that a flourishing market developed on the other side of the river. Durham market place is strategically placed between two ancient bridges, Elvet Bridge (built in 1106) and Framwellgate Bridge and has been saved from the usual fate of such a siting by the creation of a bypass. Today it has a new lease of life, benignly presided over by a statue of Lord Londonderry who created Seaham Harbour. The village of Elvet on the banks of the river was the spot to which Cuthbert's monks brought his tomb, but evidently they preferred the greater safety presented by the cliff and built their first wooden church upon it.

Durham is, in effect, two quite separate cities: the medieval city, clamped onto that great bluff, and the largely eighteenth-century city that developed on the open banks of the river when military protection was no longer a primary consideration. With no less than seven main roads converging upon it, the demands of modern traffic could have destroyed it but, partly through that intractable site, partly through a high level of imaginative town planning, much of the 'sub-urban' city has been spared. The ancient centre has always been free of traffic, but pedestrianization has spread to Silver Street, contributing to the success of the market place. Even the shopping centre, which in so many historic towns is a dreary ziggurat, won an award for design.

The steep gorge that all but surrounds the town provides some stunning views of what Walter Scot called 'part church of God, part castle 'gainst the Scots'. But it was the nineteenth-century railway engineers who provided the twentieth century with the most spectacular view of the city. The railway swoops past the city on a great viaduct and from it, for about a minute, the traveller has an unforgettable glimpse of the sandstone cathedral with its grim companion, the castle, rising up from the tree-lined gorge of the Wear.

KENDAL, CUMBRIA

'Valley of the hillstream' *Anglo-Saxon*
Population: 23,411 *Market:* Wednesday, Saturday

CERTAIN towns acquire facile topographical labels that seem to have little relevance to the locality around them. But the accuracy of Kendal's label, 'gateway to the Lakes', is only too obvious in the summer months as the streams of traffic from south and west converge and pound up Highgate, bound for Windermere and the delights beyond. On a wet day another label, 'auld grey town', is also depressingly accurate for Kendal is built of a grey limestone that darkens rapidly with moisture. But, by the same token, it comes to life with sunshine so that the whole aspect of the town can change in an instant.

'Wool is my bread' is the town's motto. It is one which could be claimed by a score of English towns, grown fat on the fleece of the sheep but it has particular relevance to Kendal. The wool industry was established here in 1331 and the town became famous for 'Kendal Green', mentioned by Shakespeare. Its prosperity is immediately evident in the immense size of the church, just 3 feet narrower than York Minster and the widest but one of all English parish churches. The Flemish aisle is a relic of those industrious weavers who, almost involuntarily, created so much capital for their host towns. Wool is evident again in the name of some of the localities – Tenterfield, Tenterbank, Tenterholme – where cloth was stretched on tenterhooks to dry.

Dr Manning's Yard. On a sunny day the 'auld grey town' looks anything but sombre as the sunlight plays on the silver-brown stones.

And wool is probably responsible for one of the most distinctive parts of Kendal's townscape, the 'yards', which run diagonally from the High Street down to the River Kent which meanders through the town. As it is possible to close off these yards it was once assumed that they were intended for defence, a reasonable assumption in a border town. However, it is more probable that their design allowed their inmates maximum access to the water which was used in such quantities in the clothing industry. There used to be about 150 of these yards but, in the post-war passion for classifying as a 'slum' any building that was old-fashioned or dilapidated and hastening to sweep it away, Kendal lost most of these distinctive features. A few, however, have been preserved – the best of them is the one known as Dr Manning's Yard opposite the New Inn – and they are worth seeking out for the view they give into the past.

There was a Roman fort at Watercrook, about half a mile south of the town, evidence that the Romans, too, were obliged to use this highway into Westmorland. But because it was purely a defensive fort, it fell into disuse after its military function ceased and the small settlement that had grown up around it moved northwards, a common sequence of events in the establishment of post-Roman towns. Roman legacies in Kendal, however, are the two distinct castle sites known respectively as Castle Howe and Castle Hill. These would have been Roman watchcamps just north of the fort proper and were subsequently developed.

Castle Howe was probably never more than a timber building, the earthworks alone surviving today, but the Normans built one of their vast stone castles on the other prominence. This had become ruinous by the end of the sixteenth century but has a particular place in English royal history for it was here that Catherine Parr, sixth and last wife of Henry VIII, was born in 1512. She was thirty-two when she was obliged to marry Henry, a late age for that period, but with maturity came the skill that enabled her to survive her murderous husband. She died, widowed for the second time, at the age of thirty-six and Kendal Town Hall reverently shel-

The Shambles. All market towns had a place set aside where butchers could carry out their unpleasant tasks. Kendal's shambles have been attractively restored to house modern shops.

ters her prayer book in which she records her innermost sad thoughts.

The ebullient Town Hall is late Victorian in style, its most distinctive feature being the complex, and rather beautiful carillon played every three hours during the day. Highgate itself is an impressive street, both curving and ascending so that, standing at the bottom, one cannot quite see the top. In changing its name to Stricklandgate half-way along, the street seems to be following the irritating English custom of change for change's sake. But this change has a topographical origin which can still be detected: for over 300 years a massive building, which had no other name than New Biggin or 'new building', closed the upper end of Highgate. It was demolished in 1803, one of the victims of growing traffic throughout the country.

'Development' has left its scars upon the town but there is still a sturdy infrastructure of historic buildings. The oldest is undoubtedly the Castle Dairy in William Street, a well-preserved example of Tudor vernacular architecture in use from Catherine Parr's time onward, though functioning now as a restaurant. A similar survivor is the Old Fleece Inn, a seventeenth-century inn which, like the Fleece at Cirencester attests the importance of the town's main industry. Sepulchre Lane is still cobbled and from it there is an excellent view of the town which permits the observer to detect the shape of the yards. And an undoubted modern asset is the development of the so-called New Shambles. The butchers' shops were moved here in the nineteenth century (hence the adjective) and have recently been turned into an attractive shopping precinct, an imaginative (and economically viable) use for outmoded buildings.

KESWICK, CUMBRIA

'Cheese farm' Anglo-Saxon
Population : 5635 Market : Saturday

ONE of the many idiosyncrasies surrounding the supposedly irreligious English is that a remarkably large number of their towns owe their founding, or at least their siting to a saint. Keswick is linked, immemorably, with the hamlet of Crossthwaite, where a certain St Kentigern planted a cross; the more romantically inclined citizens of Keswick, disliking the down-to-earth derivation of their town's name given above, argue that it should indeed be 'St Kentigern's place'.

But whatever its spiritual origins, it owed its wealth to a very practical cause: the presence of minerals in the nearby hills. The Romans had spotted this fact as soon as they had gained a foothold in the North: one can trace evidence of their interest over miles of rough country, testifying to the economic value of the lead and graphite they

The poet, Robert Southey, came to Keswick in 1803 – part of the vanguard of the 'Lakists'. He is buried in the churchyard of Great Crossthwaite close by.

extracted and sent off to the Mediterranean.

The miners came late to Keswick, very late. The town had been developed by the monks of Fountains Abbey as early as 1120, but it was not until the reign of Elizabeth I that certain gentlemen in London, prominent courtiers among them, formed a Company of Mines Royal to exploit the area. They imported 500 German miners, most of whom set up their homes in the small hamlet of Keswick and all went very well indeed. By the 1600s the operation was earning the company some £15,000 a year, a staggering sum for the time and far surpassing the value of any other natural product in the area. There was a slight embarrassment when Henry Percy, the fiery 8th earl of Northumberland, complained that Elizabeth was taking too big a share of the royalties and he was foolish enough actually to take her to court. He was imprisoned in the Tower and died in 'mysterious circumstances' while the mining industry went happily on.

In due course, mining became unprofitable (the hills, indeed, appear to have been denuded of trees so greedy for fuel were the smelters – a wearisomely familiar sequence of events). In 1648 Cromwell abolished the royal monopoly, but that could not restore an exhausted natural product and Keswick withdrew into itself, having nothing to offer would-be investors.

Nothing tangible, that is. What it did possess was a spectacular natural setting. Until the late eighteenth century, this meant nothing at all to anybody. To the contrary, the more articulate travellers in what was to be known as the Lake District warned all others from this harsh, unpredictable, dangerous, barbaric countryside. Then the cult of the 'Picturesque' began to see beauty where none before existed and, hard on its heels, William Wordsworth and his fellow 'Lakers' discovered this dramatic scenery. Samuel Taylor Coleridge settled in a large house called Greta Hall and was joined, in 1803, by Robert Southey. The Lake District industry was born as sophisticated southerners journeyed north to rub shoulders with the famous poets and discovered, in their turn, that there was indeed beauty in the hills.

*'Musical stones', formed from local aluminium silicate, are
housed in Keswick's tiny museum, along with a model of the
Lake District and manuscripts of the poets.*

*Keswick's Moot Hall is in the main street, which also
doubles as a market place. Though built only in 1813, its
foundations are sixteenth century.*

Keswick, therefore, after earning its living by the
most practical means possible, began to flourish
again, but this time through that most intangible
and subjective of concepts, the appreciation of

natural beauty. Inevitably the town became more
and more a 'tourist' locality. Yet, curiously, it did
not lose contact with its roots, certainly not in the
way that Windermere was destined to do. Around
the market place the narrow courts and alleys where
the miners had lived continue to put a dour impress
upon the town. The Moot Hall, rearing up starkly in
the middle of the market place looks workmanlike.
The shops remain attractively old-fashioned: it is
still not unheard of for chairs to be provided for
customers while assistants scurry around at their
service. It owes its survival, perhaps, to the fact that
it is a centre for mountain and fell climbers, an
austere species of tourist whose spartan needs are
less destructive of townscapes than others of their
kind.

Keswick has one other, slightly odd claim to
fame: the invention of 'musical stones'. A form of
locally occurring aluminium silicate, these stones
give a musical note when struck. In 1785 a certain
Peter Crossthwaite laid his small claim to immor-
tality when he discovered that it was possible to
arrange these stones to form a chromatic scale. The
craze took over in the nineteenth century when
owners of ever larger collections of stones toured the
country rather like the skiffle groups of the 1960s.
There is an example of one of these 'instruments' in
Keswick's tiny museum.

Keswick lies at the head of a great valley, much of it occupied by Derwentwater, one of the largest

lakes of the Lake District. This view, at once dramatic and picturesque, attracted the Lakist poets.

RICHMOND, NORTH YORKSHIRE

'Wealthy hill' French
Population: 7731 Market: Saturday

THE heart of Richmond is an immense, unspoiled, medieval market place, cobbled, and with the surrounding houses keeping their distance like spectators around an arena. At its centre is an obelisk, built in 1771 but replacing an earlier market cross erected in Henry VI's reign. This earlier cross was a massive structure (with provision, incidentally, for the public flogging of criminals) reflecting the fact that this was the largest and wealthiest corn market in northern England. So important was it to the town that the mayor's title was Clerk of the Market and even now, on market day, two halberds are displayed outside his residence.

No shops have encroached on this space as usually happens. What they have done, however, is to encroach on the church. This shares the centre of the market place with the obelisk, and the north aisle was actually used to accommodate stalls. Holy Trinity Church has had a varied history: built in 1150, but substantially rebuilt in 1360 and again in 1439, it has been used as a warehouse, school, town hall and assize court, and is currently a museum. But its curfew bell is still rung at 8 pm and, rather more unusually, at 8 am the following morning when it is known as the 'prentice bell' summoning apprentices to work.

Facing the square is the town's oldest surviving inn, the Bishop Blaize Hotel. Named after the patron saint of woolcombers, it seems to have acted as the headquarters of the knitting industry, once the town's major trade. The first pair of stockings made here was reputedly given to Elizabeth I.

John Leland, the Tudor topographer, remarked of Richmond that it is a 'towne that standith on Unequal Ground' and depending upon one's approach to it, one can actually be in the town for some

Richmond, surrounded even today by the wild countryside of Yorkshire, is dominated by its castle, impregnable on three sides and protected on its fourth side by a 90-foot high, twelfth-century keep.

Although the River Swale looks innocent and sylvan here, it was to hold this river valley that Richmond's great castle was built – and the town was built to serve the castle.

The immense market place, cobbled and enclosed by buildings that span many centuries.
The eighteenth-century obelisk replaced an earlier market cross.

time without realizing that it has one of the most stupendous ruined castles in England. The best view of this is from the south, across the beautiful stone bridge that seems to swoop across the tumbling, rushing River Swale. On this south side a cliff, now tree covered, rears up from the river and, crowning it, are the remains of the once towering castle. Of Norman origin, it was begun about 1071 and, like Ludlow and Barnard Castle, the town started life as an appendage to it: certainly it did not get a town wall of its own until 1312. Although in ruins by the eighteenth century, some of the castle's internal buildings survive to give an idea of its original function and size. A similar legend is told about it as is told about Charlemagne and Frederic Barbarossa. A local man, called Potter Thomson, is supposed to have discovered a vast underground hall beneath the castle where he found King Arthur and his knights asleep around a stone table.

New development at Richmond is mostly on the flat eastern side (and, alas, on the once open hills to the north). But the steep southern and western sides remain completely unspoiled. From the bridge the steep, cobbled Cornforth Hill leads to the market place through an old archway; the river is easily accessible, continuing in intimate association with the town so that the walker can either continue on into the valley of the Swale or climb up into the old town. The varying levels of the ground give an exhilarating variety of views: now one is walking down one of the long, narrow passages known as 'wynds', now emerging into open but urban spaces, now suddenly seeing open country framed in a ruined window or in a still intact archway. And while most of the town is medieval, one of its most outstanding attractions is the tiny Georgian theatre. There are only two others like it in England. Built in 1787 at the suggestion of a touring actor manager, Samuel Butler (one of his cast was the future star Edmund Kean), the theatre enjoyed a vigorous life until the mid nineteenth century. It was used for various inglorious purposes until 1960 when an appeal was launched for its restoration. It was reopened in 1962 as a living theatre but with an interior that exactly reproduces its original appearance two centuries ago.

RIPON, NORTH YORKSHIRE

'The Hrype tribe' Anglo-Saxon
Population: 11,952 Market: Thursday

THIS is one of England's engaging idiosyncrasies: a city, complete with immense cathedral, that is the metropolis of its region, yet not much bigger than a village. (Wells in Somerset is an even smaller example.)

The city's most famous custom is the extraordinary nightly ritual of the wakeman sounding curfew on his horn, a ritual which has almost certainly been unbroken for a thousand years. On many a wet night it has been blown in the Studley Arms, an ancient inn on the market place, not a stone's throw from the obelisk where the wakeman usually performs this custom, the market place being honoured in spirit if not quite in substance.

The curfew originally had a prosaic significance: if a citizen was burgled after the watch was set the wakeman was obliged both to pay compensation and catch the burglar. In the town's regalia there are today two horns, the original Charter Horn of 886 and the Millenary Horn, marking the first thousand years of the custom. In 1976, the Bicentenary of the American Declaration of Independence, the ancient town sent decorated horns to two of its American namesakes, the towns of Ripon, Wisconsin and Ripon, California.

The market place rivals that of Richmond in size, being some two acres overall. As in Richmond, the ancient Market Cross was replaced in 1781 by the existing obelisk. The market played a vital economic role in the town's history, though its lucrative tolls were firmly in the hands of the church, going initially to the archbishop of York as lord of the manor and then, when the cathedral was established in 1836, to the bishop of Ripon. It was not until 1880 that the city gained control, paying £1500 for the privilege. It had, however, always been able to levy

Ripon Cathedral. One of England's few remaining Saxon crypts, believed to have been built by St Wilfrid in 672, lies below the cathedral. It is now a strong-room holding church treasures.

Despite the age of the city, the Town Hall is relatively modern, having been built in 1799. The Wakeman was the principal officer, equivalent to the mayor.

enough, used it as their headquarters until 1950, when it passed into private ownership. The sixteenth-century Wakeman's House in the market place has the rather unreal look of a building that has been too enthusiastically restored, but it is the authentic home of the last wakeman. This was Hugh Ripley who was instrumental in obtaining the town's first royal charter as a borough in 1604 and, in consequence, became its first mayor. And down by the river is the calm and dignified Thorpe

For perhaps a thousand years the Wakeman has been 'setting the watch' in Ripon as night approaches. The ceremony now takes place at 9 pm in the market place.

tolls on the corn market and though this no longer exists, the town's bellman rings his bell on market day to signify the official opening of the general market.

Despite its comparatively recent elevation as the seat of a bishop, Ripon Cathedral is probably as old as the town. The Saxon saint, Wilfrid, built a church here and the Normans preserved its crypt when they built their own church. This in turn was rebuilt by Archbishop Roger of York (a contemporary, but most certainly no friend of Thomas à Becket). The west front, the most distinctive part of the building, was built about 1220 and, in the opinion of Nikolaus Pevsner, is the most important example of early Gothic in England.

The town possesses a remarkable number of historic buildings, not only those now recognized as of architectural importance, but late nineteenth-century buildings that have long since disappeared in other towns. The Workhouse in Allhallowgate, for instance, was built in 1854 on the site of an older example and is now a rather attractive feature, and the House of Correction, which served as the town's prison from its erection in 1813 until 1878, is also still evident. The County Police, appropriately

Prebend House, mostly early seventeenth century with considerable Victorian alterations. It is a distinct feather in Ripon's cap that its energetic Civic Society acts as a watchdog over the town's architectural heritage.

The topographical reason for Ripon's establishment – relative ease of access – threatens it today as the vast new roads come ever closer. But it shows no disrespect to Ripon to say also that one of its attractions is the ease with which one can leave it behind: down the steps, past the cathedral and within moments one has gained the open river and miles of towpath.

SKIPTON, NORTH YORKSHIRE

'Sheep farm' *Anglo-Saxon*
Population : 13,246 *Market :* Monday, Wednesday, Friday, Saturday *Cattle :* Monday

THERE is a solid, comfortable, no-nonsense, very Yorkshire air about Skipton. Its historic and architectural attractions are not immediately evident as in Richmond or Ludlow, although they indubitably exist. What the visitor does see immediately is a small rural capital going busily about its affairs. The endless, thunderous, brutal traffic has driven the cattle market from the wide, handsome High Street which was its home for centuries. But the general market still takes place there, the local townsfolk shopping for their pies, vegetables and cheeses a hair's-breadth from titans careering past. Tourism is taking the place of the light industries that were the town's staple source of wealth, but at least it keeps the fascinating canal system alive, and the broad vowels of Yorkshire still effortlessly dominate conversations in pubs and restaurants.

Sheep farming was the reason for the town's origin back in the seventh century, and still substantially contributes to its affluence: on one market day in 1976 sheep to a value of £130,000 changed hands. By the time the Norman tax-gatherers came round in 1086, assessing the wealth of the kingdom, the settlement's chief function as a market for the

The gateway of Skipton Castle with the Clifford motto 'Desormais' above it. Its owner, Lady Anne Clifford, substantially rebuilt it after its Cromwellian destruction.

The courtyard of Skipton Castle with the immense old yew tree and an ancient font taken from St James's chapel.

sheep pastured on the surrounding hills was so well established that its name entered history as 'Sciptone'. And in due course a fleece appeared on its coat-of-arms.

The Industrial Revolution treated the town kindly, bringing in modest prosperity but not overwhelming the place with factories and mines. The population shot up from 2305 in 1801 to 5044 in 1852, receiving yet another boost to nearly 10,000 when the railway came. But the town was already solidly rooted enough to cope with the expansion without losing its identity, small streets of elegant Georgian houses, the great Norman castle and the canal between them providing a framework.

The Victorian town hall in the High Street is a product of the years of expansion. Its predecessor, the old Toll Booth, is tucked away in Middle Row, just off the High Street. This block is almost certainly a classic example of market-place encroachment. Here was the true nucleus of the town, the site of the Moot Hall. The ancient Court of Pie Powder, the regulating authority for the market, and the town's own Court Leet (a manorial, as opposed to King's Court) used this as their headquarters. Subsequently, the Toll Booth became the town's parliament, from the sixteenth until the late nineteenth century, and also the home of the Mechanics' Institute, that determined example of self-help launched by the Yorkshireman, Birkbeck, in the nineteenth century. Skipton, with a curious lack of civic pride, permitted this historic building to become a restaurant but, reportedly, the prison cells are still extant.

Agriculture brought the town into being but the castle gave it status and shape – the triangular area in front of it at the top of the High Street marks the original market place. The castle's siting is notable: the entrance from the High Street is on the same plane, but by walking round to the delightful forested area known as Skipton Woods one can see from below the massive sandstone rock upon which the Normans sited the original building. Much of the present structure was the work of Robert de Romillé in the early fourteenth century and, in

Springs canal. This waterway provided the town's industrial lifeblood in the nineteenth century.

common with most royalist strongholds, was 'slighted', or substantially dismantled after the Civil War. But the parliamentarians had reckoned without its redoubtable chatelaine, Lady Anne Clifford (see also Appleby, p. 131). Telling Cromwell to his face 'that if he pulled her castles about her ears she would build them up again as fast', she set about rebuilding the family seat and within three years, by 1658, had restored it to the condition that it is in today. It is the perfect example of an early medieval fortress that has been adapted to residential use by Tudor and Jacobean hands.

The parish church that immediately adjoins the castle was probably once within its grounds. Cer-

Skipton's market place shares the broad High Street with traffic. In the background is the Toll Booth, predecessor to the Victorian Town Hall.

tainly, they seem to have been so closely associated that Lady Anne gave it priority in repairing the damage it, too, had suffered as a result of the war: 'In the summer of 1655, at her own charge she caus'd the steeple of Skipton Church to be built up againe, that was pulled down in the time of the late Warrs (and) raised up a noble Tomb of Black Marble in memory of her Warlike Father.' The nineteenth century was kinder to this church than many. The sixteenth-century rood loft has gone, replaced by the present reredos designed by the ubiquitous Giles Gilbert Scott, but the superb oaken roof is an ecclesiastical gem, mostly of the fourteenth and fifteenth centuries. A stone's throw from the church is perhaps an even more exceptional survival, the High Corn Mill. For at least 800 years, from the late twelfth century until the 1950s, there has been a working mill on this site. A local corn merchant bought the mill in 1964 and began the extensive work of restoration, turning it not simply into a museum but, again, into a working mill – with a bonus. A water turbine produces electricity for the mill, thus using modern technology to keep alive an old tradition.

It is now used mostly by pleasure craft.

THE BORDERS

APPLEBY, CUMBRIA

'Apple village' *Anglo-Saxon*
Population: 2380 *Market:* Saturday *Cattle:* Monday, Friday

THIS is a town as delightful and as fresh as its name which, unlike so many place-names, really means what it indicates: the first settlement here was truly an apple-producing village. One's first impression is of greenness for the River Eden (what better name for a river in such an idyllic setting) coils round the little town in a vast protective loop and between river and town are broad, lush water meadows. The traveller crosses a sandstone bridge over the shallow, sparkling, swift-moving river and comes immediately into the heart of the town.

It seems, at first sight, like an immense stage set in which the spectator is part of the play. Ahead lies a broad, gently rising street – so broad, indeed, that it

This aerial view, taken from immediately above the castle, looks down Boroughgate towards the Moot Hall. The pillar in front of the castle is the High Cross.

appears to be that formal open space so much used by Continentals, originating as the forum and now called *piazza*, *place* or *platz*, but for which the English do not even have a name. In most other towns this would be known as the High Street; in Appleby it is the Boroughgate and is all but enclosed. At the bottom is the church of St Lawrence behind its garden and stone screen; at the top is the great castle behind its own screen of high wall and trees. Breaking the otherwise clear vista is the Moot Hall. It looks a typical Georgian building but it dates from 1596 and was refaced and given its black and white finish in the eighteenth century.

Appleby was born of the castle. In that tremendous upsurge of building after the Conquest, the invading Normans planted castles all along these north-western marches. The site of Appleby was a natural defensive position; like Durham, but on a smaller scale, the builders found a steep hill protected by the loop of the river. In the sixteenth century the formidable Lady Anne Clifford extended and developed the castle during the great face-lift she gave to all the Clifford possessions in the North (see also Skipton, p. 129). Not only did she restore the castle between 1651 and 1665 but she also gave the town its handsome almshouses, called after her namesake St Anne, which are one of the features of the Boroughgate.

The town enters history in its own right in 1120 when the Earl of Chester granted it to the abbey of St Mary at York. It was still merely an appendage to the castle, not even deserving a name of its own. But it soon became a prize worth having for the Scots seized it in 1174, declaring that they would occupy it 'until the Day of Judgement'. Evidently the Day of Judgement took place the following year, for the English recaptured it then and never lost it again.

The town has actually declined in population since the Middle Ages for it would have been around 2500 in the 1390s. A result of that decline has been the preservation of what is essentially a twelfth-century town plan. Parallel with the Boroughgate, and with only two entrances into it, is the splendidly named Doomsgate, which leads via Scattergate along the side of the castle, over the river to the town mill and to Bongate. This would have been the 'apple village', the original site of the town. Bongate, now mostly a green area quite distinct in character from the rest of the town, was where the peasants or bondsmen lived, as distinct from the free citizens – the burgesses – who lived in and around the

burgessgate (Boroughgate). Even today, an aerial photograph clearly shows the burgage plots, those long, narrow strips of land behind each house that are a distinctive feature of an historic English town.

Appleby boasts two crosses, the nineteenth-century Low Cross at the bottom of the hill and the smaller, older High Cross which marks both the site of the ancient market place as well as the limit of Boroughgate. A motto carved upon it neatly sums up the double meaning of a free citizenry living under the shadow of an enormous castle: 'Retain your Loyalty: Preserve your Rights'. The famous cheese market used to be held here and though this has gone the way of most specialized markets, Appleby still holds no less than three market days a week – remarkable in so tiny a town and indicative of its social importance in this wild and remote countryside.

Appleby was also the centre for a number of annual fairs, of which the so-called New Fair (actually established by charter in 1685) is the sole survivor. But this flourishes on a remarkable scale with its emphasis on horse trading. It lasts from Thursday to the following Wednesday, beginning in the first week of June, and people are attracted to it from all over England, gypsies in particular. Horse trading is still an important activity, usually concentrated on the Tuesday, but the rumbustious week-long carnival atmosphere is appealing more and more to spectators and participants, rather than traders.

Britain's largest horsefair is still held in this tiny Cumbrian town every June.

BERWICK-ON-TWEED, NORTHUMBERLAND

'Corn farm on the River Tweed' *Anglo-Saxon*
Population: 11,610 *Market:* Wednesday, Saturday *Cattle:* Saturday

BERWICK is rich in the eccentric anomalies that the British love to preserve. The town lies in England, but its county is in Scotland. Its population is not much more than that of a large village, but at one time it was virtually a city-state of a kind common in Italy yet all but unknown in Britain. Officially styled 'The County of the Borough and Town of Berwick-upon-Tweed', until 1746 it had to be specifically mentioned in any act of parliament relating to the affairs of England and Scotland. Indeed, the locals claim to be still legally at war with Russia as the peace treaty which brought the Crimean War to an end did not in fact mention this border town.

It is, of course, its position on the border between England and Scotland that is not only responsible for the historical idiosyncracies but also much of its physical appearance, in particular the mighty fortifications that make a visit to the town essential for any student of military architecture. In the endless struggle between England and Scotland it changed hands thirteen times. The town saw some of the bloodiest fighting in that brutal rivalry between the English and Scottish kings: Edward I slaughtered some 7000 townsfolk after the rebellion of John Balliol and later exposed the Countess of Buchan for years in an open cage in the castle as punishment for her part in the crowning of Robert Bruce.

It is perhaps symbolic that the first of the three great bridges that cross the Tweed here was built by the first Anglo-Saxon king, James I of England (also James VI of Scotland as the Scots are at pains to point out). According to legend, James had difficulty crossing the original rickety wooden structure that spanned the wide estuary when on his way to claim the English crown in 1603. Certainly, it was the King's Surveyor, James Burrell, who built what

The bridges of Berwick. In the foreground is the seventeenth-century Old Bridge with its fifteen arches, and in the distance Stephenson's nineteenth-century Royal Border bridge. Between them is the modern road bridge, opened in 1928.

Salmon fishing, once a major commercial activity, still takes place though on a reduced scale.

is now known as the Old Bridge, an astonishing structure of some fifteen arches that, despite its complete lack of elegance, has a great presence. So well did Burrell build the bridge that it carried the Great North Road until 1928, when the present Royal Tweed Bridge (a concrete construction as impressive in its way) replaced it. Further upstream is Robert Stephenson's Royal Border Bridge, a railway bridge that could visually do duty for a Roman aqueduct.

Berwick's walls are outstanding not simply for England, but for all Europe. Mostly they are the product of Elizabeth I's reign, and the extent of her fear of a Franco-Scottish invasion is well shown by the money which this most niggardly of monarchs poured out for the construction of a set of fortifications designed to withstand the formidable onslaught of contemporary artillery. Instead of high, relatively narrow walls supported by towers, the new defence demanded low, extremely solid structures backed up by earth-fills. Ironically, Elizabeth's expensive defences were never used in war. Indeed, the only military damage they ever experienced occurred when they were used as the target for Bren-gun practice in World War II.

The impenetrable bulk of the walls ensured their survival and they, in turn, contained and defined the town within. Nikolaus Pevsner, not a man to scatter compliments, described it as 'One of the most exciting towns in England, a real town with a strong sense of enclosure, a town of red roofs and grey houses with hardly an irritating line anywhere and a town of the most intricate change of levels.' Those sheltering walls provide the perfect platform from which a sauntering visitor can view the changing panorama of the town.

Salmon fishing is still, happily, an important local industry. The Norfolk writer, George Borrow, left one of the most vivid portrayals of this event in the mid nineteenth century. Describing the force of the greenish water pouring through the arches of the Old Bridge he continues: 'There were songs upon the river from the fisher barks, and occasionally a chorus plaintive and wild such as I had never heard before. Several robust fellows were near me, some knee-deep in water, employed in hauling the sieve upon the sand. Huge fish were struggling among the meshes – princely salmon – their brilliant mail of blue and silver flashing in the morning beam.' But Berwick has also had to face the problem that most English ports and harbours now face as patterns of

Market day in Berwick. The Toll Booth or Town Hall was built in the mid nineteenth century, its top floor once serving as the local gaol.

transport change, and once busy port and dockyard areas become derelict. The city fathers resisted the temptation to erase Berwick's disused harbour site with a bulldozer. Instead, a flexible and imaginative programme of restoration and highly selective demolition is turning it into a lively tourist attraction.

This ancient town is dominated by a relatively late building, that of the elegant Town Hall built in 1757 and strongly influenced in design by London's St Martin-in-the-Fields. It closes the end of the attractive High Street, the only wide street in a town of deliberately narrow lanes and passages known locally as 'closes'. This was the site both of the market and the fairs that once produced much of the town's wealth. Along the narrow lanes leading to the river one can still see the great warehouses and granaries that stored the goods traded in the market place, a tradition which has been maintained throughout the centuries. Other customs that have been cherished are the May fair, which takes place on the last Friday of the month, the Tweedmouth Feast (mid-July) and the Running of the Walls Race (September).

HEXHAM, NORTHUMBERLAND

'Warriors' estate' Anglo-Saxon
Population : 9630 *Market :* Tuesday

THERE could scarcely be a better name than 'warriors' estate' for this charming but tough little town – less than 3 miles away is Hadrian's Wall, beyond which lay only barbarism and night. The first view of the town from the north is from the Signing Bank, so-called because travellers, seeing the safety promised by the town, supposedly crossed themselves in gratitude for their escape from the Scots. The town lies at the very hub of that Border country whose endless, bloody disputes, expressed as cattle-stealing or fought out in battle, continued well into modern times. Its position brought prosperity as well as bloodshed. From the early eighteenth century onwards, cattle bred in Scotland would be driven south to the great cattle market held in the town. Bought by local graziers, they would be fattened on the lusher grass of northern England.

Wilfrid, bishop of York, received the locality as a gift from the strong-minded Ethelreda. Married to a king of Northumbria, she retained her virginity at all costs, and finally became abbess of Ely, adding insult to her husband's injury by passing over her lands to her spiritual father, Wilfrid. From this arose that ill-defined, but very real 'kingdom' known as the 'regality of Hexham', in its tiny way not dissimilar to those States of the Church in Italy which made of the Pope a landed magnate. Certainly this was Wilfrid's interpretation of the gift and he set about building a priory at the centre of Hexham.

Only the crypt of Wilfrid's church remains. But this is almost intact, reaching back through centuries that even predate Wilfrid, for much of the stone was obtained from the Roman garrison town of Corstopitum. The existence of the crypt was totally forgotten until 1725 when a workman fell into it.

Up above, in the nave of the existing building, is one of the most poignant of Roman memorials, the tombstone of a 25-year-old standard bearer, Flavinius. He belonged to the crack cavalry regiment known as the Ala Petriana, stationed at Corstopitum, and presumably met his death in action for his tombstone shows him as a mounted soldier riding down a barbarian. Not far from this pagan monument is the throne or chair of St Wilfrid,

Saxon and Roman remains jostle each other within Hexham Abbey. This is the tombstone of the Roman standard bearer, Flavinius, who was probably based nearby.

known as the Frith Stool, which has been moved restlessly from one place to another around the church.

The Danes totally destroyed the church above ground in 875. Looking back, one is always surprised by the degree of destruction achieved by these pirates who, no matter how dedicated they were to their task, were necessarily limited by time and the intractable nature of their material. Fire would account for the destruction of the wooden areas; stone, however, is difficult to burn. A clue as to the cause of the rest of the damage is provided by

Hexham Market, on the high plateau in the heart of the town with the abbey in the background.

the presence, all around the town, of ancient stone-work appearing in buildings of a lesser age. The townsfolk of Hexham, it seems, were untroubled by piety when a supply of ready-hewn stone was available. The main structure of Hexham Priory dates now from the twelfth century, but it is difficult to believe that its Saxon predecessor could have surpassed this superb building. Even after the Dissolution, and further plundering of its stone, it forms the very heart of the town, linked to it both physically and socially.

Hexham stands on a platform above the River Tyne and its principle buildings are clustered around the market place which crowns the platform. Along the southern side is an elegant covered market place, built in 1766 and known inelegantly as the Shambles. Apart from the priory, whose great buildings and green spaces form the western side,

the dominant feature is the Moot Hall, a fourteenth-century structure which curiously resembles a forti-fied Italian *palazzo municipale* – an indication of the violence of life in this locality. Nearby is the Manor Office, equally massive in size and erected as a prison in 1330. It owes its name to the fact that the business of the manor was transacted here from Tudor times until 1867. Both buildings, immense though they are, formed only a fragment of the vast castle of the bishop of York, which held that splendidly named 'regality of Hexham'. Moot Hall and Manor Office have been given a new lease of life, now sympathetically adapted for use as a tourist centre and museum respectively. The Manor Office also has an excellent display interpreting the social life of the Border country, that combination of cattle-stealing, brawling and feudal loyalties that lingered on here long after it left the rest of England.

CHEPSTOW, GWENT

'Market place' *Anglo-Saxon*
Population: 9309 *Market:* occasional

It is worthwhile travelling to Chepstow from the south, preferably by train, to experience the notable contrast in urban development. From Newport, itself a chaos of traffic problems and bad planning, the train passes through a drab, light-industrial landscape, reaching its nadir at Chepstow station. A dreary Station Road seems to lead nowhere in particular, leaving the visitor to wonder why he has bothered to come to this town. The road climbs a hill – and suddenly the traveller is precipitated into one of the most delightful town centres, its steeply ascending High Street enclosed at its summit by a massive stone gate. This contrast between Chepstow's historic core and its modern approaches illustrates perfectly the fact that the twentieth century, whatever its technological achievements, has lost the art of town building.

Strictly speaking, the inclusion of Chepstow in a book on English market towns should ensure its burning by the common hangman on the steps of Cardiff Town Hall for it is technically in Wales. As you cross the elegant stone bridge over the muddy, turbulent Wye a sign welcomes you to England. But this is the result of the 1974 Local Government Act, which attempted to determine whether Monmouth belongs to Wales or England.

The Normans, who built the vast castle here the year following the Battle of Hastings, struggled for some time to call the place by its original Welsh name, turning it into 'Striguil' or 'Estighoiel'. But its importance as a market place ensured that, by 1306, its Saxon name of Chepstow was universally used and its ambience today is purely English.

This is one of Britain's very few small, walled towns. The Portwall, extending from the castle in a sweeping semi-circle, defines and still contains the nucleus of the town. It looks impressive, a good 6 feet thick and 15 feet high, but in fact it has no foundation and a cannonade would have laid it flat. Built about 1275, its primary purpose would have been to facilitate the collection of tolls for, as the name 'Portwall' suggests, Chepstow owed much of its affluence to the fact that it was a port. As early as 1086 the Domesday Book recorded that William fitz Osbern, who had built the castle, received forty

FORM OF THE
CEREMONY
FOR OPENING
CHEPSTOW BRIDGE,
On Wednesday, 24th July, 1816.

Company to assemble in the Square at One o'Clock.

THE PROCESSION,
A PAIR OF COLOURS.
ENGINEER & SURVEYOR.
Workmen in Divisions according to their Order, walking two and two.
A PAIR OF COLOURS.

This poster commemorates the opening of the bridge built by John Raistrick in 1816, which still carries traffic.

shillings a year from ships going upstream and his son, Roger, expanded the trade. In the Middle Ages wine and salt were major staples of the town's economy and, later, ship-building. The locals claim that the Chepstow firm of Bowsher, Hodges and Watkins supplied half of the ship-building timber used throughout the entire Napoleonic campaign.

The town reached the peak of its prosperity in the early nineteenth century. Brunel threw his great railway bridge across the river, parts of which still survive, in 1856. Further upstream John Raistrick of Bridgenorth built the present charming road bridge. The first bridge on this site was of Roman construction, and Raistrick's bridge is probably its fifth or sixth successor. The builders of all these bridges had one truly extraordinary problem: the fact that the Wye rises and falls by some 49 feet. Raistrick did his job well: this is still the only road crossing at this point, used by very heavy industrial as well as local traffic.

Perhaps a century ago, this riverside area was the very dynamo of the town, its wharfs, timber yards and brick yards extending far downstream. The inns, taverns and boarding houses that provided refreshment and shelter for the seamen and dock

The urgent necessity to defend England against the Welsh is well illustrated by the immensely strong castle. Work began upon it within a year of the Battle of Hastings.

workers crowded the area, achieving a considerable degree of notoriety. After the decline of the town as a port, it began to rise again as a tourist centre; sophisticated travellers in search of the 'picturesque' discovered the Wye valley in the early eighteenth century and Chepstow benefitted. But the riverside area was to feel the greatest effects of the decline and is only now being brought slowly back to life. An enterprising potter, Ned Heywood (who incidentally discovered that the fine Wye mud

Chepstow's market place, leading to the river.

made a superb greenish glaze), probably triggered off the process by colour washing his house exterior. Others followed and what was once a drab, derelict area now stands transformed as a web of streets with houses of great charm and distinction, the whole backed by the vast bulk of the castle.

It would be difficult to find a greater contrast than that between the southern entry to Chepstow, with its last sad reminders of a great industrial period (the station was also the work of Brunel) and the northern exit. Here, the Wye is not an attractive river, at low tide displaying acres of mud, at high tide its waters running muddy brown. But to look upstream from the bridge is to see a vista which has changed little since the Hon. John Byng described it during his 'Tour to the West' in 1781: 'Chepstow Castle now display'd itself most superbly, placed on the very edge of the rock. The ruins seemed very magnificent. The bridge, lower down, is built very lightly of wood and covered only by planks to yield to the strong tides, which sometimes rise fifty feet.' There can be few beauty spots in England which look much the same either in an eighteenth-century engraving or a twentieth-century photograph.

LUDLOW, SALOP

'Hill by the rapid' *Anglo-Saxon*
Population: 7569 *Market:* Friday, Saturday *Cattle:* Monday

FROM Ludlow's tiny railway station you can not only hear, but smell the cattle market in action. Those few towns in England that still boast cattle markets have primly banished them to the outskirts. Not so Ludlow: despite the elegance of its architecture and its fashionable ambience (the Festival brings in thousands of people each year), its cattle market lies just off the very centre of the town. It is still privately administered, handling some 8000 head of cattle and 25,000 sheep annually. Nor does all the produce go down to the Great Wen, as William Cobbett once complained. The town still has its small butchers' shops, interspersed with shops that sell nothing but the superb local pies. And though they no longer bid for butter in the elegant eighteenth-century Butter Cross it still serves as a market place.

Wool was the source of the town's medieval prosperity – and the reason why its inhabitants built such superb private houses. In this the town's topography was important, as it was built on the 'hill by the rapids'. The River Teme, surging along far below, once powered eleven mills along its length, including three of those vital fulling mills used in the preparation of woollen cloth.

Ludlow is one of England's very few planned towns, beginning life as an appendage to the great castle. The castle itself was built between 1086 and 1094, and a small market came into existence at the castle gates, largely serving the castle garrison and residents. Over the following century the town was formally laid out by the lord of the manor, still as an extension to the castle. The townsfolk provided services, and also an income as the market began to

*Ludlow's cattle market is still held
within the town precincts.*

The sixteenth-century Feathers Inn, whose façade is a masterpiece of the carpenter's art.

This general view of Ludlow shows the great castle guarding the River Teme and the soaring tower of the Parish Church of St Laurence.

develop in its own right. By 1800 there were six fairs a year, drawing in hundreds of people from many miles around, as well as the weekly Monday market. There were two flourishing local industries, glove-making and malting, which gradually made the little town economically balanced.

But the town was still dominated, socially as well as physically, by the castle, for this was the seat of the powerful Council of the Marches which ruled Wales and the Border country until 1689. Some of the town's most important buildings were erected or acquired by members of the Council. The Feathers Inn – perhaps one of the best-known of all English inns – was built by the Secretary of the Council sometime after 1558. After the decline of the castle's social role, the town became a kind of small-scale Bath with fashionable county folk erecting their town houses within the walls. Or rather, erecting a fashionable Georgian façade over a medieval frame. This is particularly evident in one of the most famous of all English urban streets, the supremely beautiful Broad Street. Over the past few years an enterprising local historical society has been gradu-

ally investigating the history of this street, covering more than 600 years.

Small industries are still important in the town's economy, but the influence of agriculture is also evident. The 6000 odd acres of Lord Plymouth's estate, Oakley Park, contain the town to the south. The road through that estate is lined with a row of young oaks, a superb gesture of confidence in the continuity of English farming, while the present cattle market (the old Bull Ring or Beast Market was built over long ago) still lies within earshot of Broad Street.

Superbly sited, generously endowed with some of England's most beautiful domestic architecture and only 30 miles from Birmingham, it seems remarkable that Ludlow has not simply become a dormitory as has happened to other towns within the gravitational pull of great cities. Its position defends the town from this threat, as it defended the town during the turbulent Middle Ages. Between Ludlow and Birmingham rise the Clee Hills. Although only 1790 feet at their highest point, their steep banks form a sufficiently formidable barrier.

ROSS-ON-WYE, HEREFORD & WORCESTER

'Little moor on the River Wye' *Welsh*
Population : 8200 *Market* : Thursday, Saturday *Cattle* : Friday

LIKE Ludlow, topography has saved Ross-on-Wye from the current English urban plague – suburban sprawl. The town sits on a steep sandstone cliff, rearing up from the water meadows of the Wye. A beautiful greensward separates the cliff from the river and over the centuries a few houses appeared along it. But because it was liable to flood, townsfolk preferred to build higher up and the green ribbon remains unscathed. Indeed, the water meadows appear to be expanding: there is a dead oak tree in the centre which, it has been calculated, began life as a sapling on the banks of the river in the mid sixteenth century.

The road winds up to the town from the river, and at the crest two alternatives face the visitor, each leading to a wholly different townscape. There is no indication that the rather ordinary right-hand road that lies off the High Street leads to an extraordinary urban complex. Ross is an architectonic town. It has a number of interesting, indeed, fascinating buildings but the picture which the visitor takes away is of the town as one vast piece of architectural sculpture – a picture enhanced by the clever floodlighting at night. This architectonic quality is seen at its best around the church. St Mary's crowns the highest point of the town but is itself girded round with green space from which one looks out over the Wye valley as from the prow of a ship. And immediately below the church, massive buildings in the local reddish sandstone – or, in the case of the black and white hotel, in timber and plaster – form a lower terrace, itself dominated by a round sandstone tower built as a folly.

The alternative route brings the visitor straight into the hurly-burly of the market place. On Thursdays and Saturdays the Market House, the town's most famous building, comes into its own with traders selling fabrics and such like vulnerable goods, gratefully taking shelter in its colonnaded ground floor. A solid oak staircase leads up to the second floor, today used as a library but which in the past served a variety of functions. In turn it has been a school, a courthouse and – to celebrate the coming of the railway in 1855 – a ballroom, testimony to the craftsmanship of its builders. Outside

market days, the market place is seen as an elegant, triangular space, the kind of place in which one would delight in loitering were it not tormented by the traffic.

The first major settlement here was probably Roman, on the site known as Ariconium about 2 miles away. In the usual manner, after the Romans had departed the newcomers preferred to settle near, rather than in the vacated town and Ross (a Celtic word which can mean moor or promontory) came into being. The bishops of Hereford had a palace here choosing to build on the high plateau, as much with an eye to security as aesthetics, and as early as the fourteenth century the town's importance as a market allowed it to send two MPs to Westminster.

William Cobbett, that eminently pragmatic, literally down-to-earth commentator on rural affairs visited the town in 1821 and gave it his accolade. 'Ross is an old-fashioned town; but it is very beautifully situated, and if there is little of *finery* in the appearance of the inhabitants, there is little of *misery*. It is a good, plain, country town or settlement of tradesmen, whose business is that of supplying the wants of cultivators of the soil.'

Cobbett had a good eye for farming, but little

The Market Hall, built in 1670.

A general view of the town, showing its position on a high bluff above the water meadows.

appreciation of style, particularly that of urban architecture. Through the disinterested activities of a remarkable citizen of the town, Ross was already famous for its appearance. The citizen was John Kyrle (christened the 'Man of Ross' by Alexander Pope in an unusually benevolent epigram), who was born in nearby Dymock in 1637 and died in Ross in 1724. The delightful view of the town from the river owes everything to him for it was he who laid out the Prospect and the causeway from the bridge up to the town. He restored the church spire, which is today the very badge of Ross, laid out an avenue of elms in the churchyard and very practically saw to the water supply. In return his descendants recorded their debt by naming innumerable streets, societies and buildings after him as well as one handsome little inn, The Man of Ross, crowned with his bust.

It was the town's beauty, and its position in the spectacular Wye valley, that was to generate much of its income. Like Chepstow, in the late eighteenth century the more cultured upper classes had begun to discover the beauties of nature – provided they conformed to the rigid canon of the 'Picturesque'. The poet Thomas Gray, who, more than any man, opened up the Lake District, came to Ross and gave it his approval, closely followed by William Words-

worth. The advent of the stagecoach at about the same time brought in well-heeled visitors eager to sample the delights of the scenery. But they also liked their creature comforts and could pay for them, and out of this demand arose Ross's superb inns, outstanding even in a region noted for them.

The Royal Hotel occupied the site of the old bishop's palace, adding its black and white features to the mosaic of buildings on the high plateau. In the High Street the King's Head, standing next to John Kyrle's old home, adapted itself to the gentry whilst leaving much untouched: a vertiginous well is still visible in one of the public rooms. The fifteenth-century Rosslyn has a vast seventeenth-century fireplace to delight present day visitors. And the nineteenth century is well represented by The Chase on the Gloucester Road. This must surely be among the very last of the merchant princes' palaces. It was built in 1815 for the Strong family of brewers and, far from being ashamed of their origin 'in trade', they proudly displayed the hops and grapes of their profession on the solid marble pillars of the entrance hall. It became a hotel in 1922. Yet the beautiful grounds survive as a miniature green belt, bringing the historic town centre to a decorous termination on its eastern edge.

GAZETTEER

THE market towns in the gazetteer that follows are equally as fascinating as the fifty towns chosen for fuller treatment in the preceding pages. Where possible the lesser known town was chosen for closer coverage (e.g. Warwick instead of Stratford-upon-Avon, Faringdon instead of Abingdon). Some twenty-five towns have been listed in gazetteer form in an attempt to provide a comprehensive and balanced survey of the English market town.

Abingdon, Oxfordshire
'Aebba's hill' *Anglo-Saxon*
Population: 22,686 *Market:* Monday
County town of Berkshire until 1870, but now within Oxfordshire's boundaries. Superb Charles II County Hall reputed to have been built by Wren's master mason, Christopher Kempster. Numerous medieval to Georgian buildings of great charm.

Alton, Hampshire
'Farm by a spring' *Anglo-Saxon*
Population: 14,646 *Market:* Tuesday
Busy little town surrounded by hopfields on the route of the Pilgrim Fathers. The church bears moving evidence of the devotion of Charles I's soldiers, falling in their king's cause, and the south door bears the bullet marks of parliamentary troops. Superb inn, White Swan.

Ampthill, Bedfordshire
'Ant-infested hill' *Anglo-Saxon*
Population: 20,760 *Market:* Thursday
This typical English country town is at its busiest on Thursdays when the market, dating from 1219, takes place. The unhappy Catherine of Aragon awaited her divorce in the now vanished castle. More recently, Kit Williams used Catherine's commemorative cross in the park as the main clue in his extraordinary treasure hunt, *Masquerade*.

Beccles, Suffolk
'Pasture in the little stream' *Anglo-Saxon*
Population: 8900 *Market:* Friday
This little town on the Waveney river is surrounded by a network of local waterways, a colourful scene in summer. Fire, that scourge of medieval towns, gutted Beccles in the sixteenth century and again in the seventeenth. Therefore mostly well preserved Georgian architecture.

Beverley, Humberside
'Beaver stream' *Anglo-Saxon*
Population: 16,433 *Market:* Saturday
Cattle: Wednesday
The Market Cross in Saturday Market and the courtroom in the Georgian Guildhall are noteworthy hallmarks of Beverley, as is the Minster with its double transepts. The North Bar, a brick structure with battlements, is the only survivor of the town's five gates.

Blandford Forum, Dorset
'Gudgeon ford with a market' *Anglo-Saxon*
Population: 12,100 *Market:* Thursday, Saturday
An attractive market town on the River Stour, Blandford Forum is another eighteenth-century town created by fire. In 1731 most of the town centre went up in flames and two local architects, John and William Bastard, created the delightfully homogenous town of today.

Dominating the market square is the town clock. The turret formerly stood on the ancient Moot Hall that once occupied this site.

Bodmin, Cornwall
'House of the monks' *Cornish*
Population: 12,148 *Market:* Saturday
On the steep south-west edge of Bodmin Moor, this town was once known for its holy wells. St Petroc founded his monastery here, hence its place-name derivation. The local granite used for Bodmin's houses is also strikingly evident in the tors which rise up from the moor.

Bury St Edmunds, Suffolk
'Fort on shrine of St Edmund' *Anglo-Saxon*
Population: 28,914 *Market:* Saturday
Cattle: Wednesday
One of England's few successful planned towns, surviving the commuter expansion of the twentieth century. Laid out in the eleventh century by a remarkable churchman, Abbot Baldwin, whose street pattern is still clear. Moyses Hall, built in 1180, is one of England's oldest Norman houses, and the town also boasts England's smallest pub.

Buxton, Derbyshire
'Logan stone' *Anglo-Saxon*
Population: 20,800 *Market:* Saturday
A little piece of Bath transported to the wilds of Derbyshire. The spa created Buxted's fame, but it was a powerful local landowner, the Duke of Devonshire, who boosted it by laying out the great Crescent in the eighteenth century.

Chichester, West Sussex
'Roman fort occupied by Cissi' *Anglo-Saxon*
Population: 24,189 *Market:* Wednesday
A perfect miniature city, complete with city walls, cathedral and exquisite Market Cross. The original Roman street plan can still be traced with ease.

Chippenham, Wiltshire
'Cippa's estate' *Anglo-Saxon*
Population: 19,290 *Market:* Friday
Chippenham has been a market community since Saxon times, when King Alfred stayed here. Despite industrial development its character remains essentially unchanged. At the centre is the market place with its twin-gabled Town Hall capped by a wooden turret.

Chipping Campden, Gloucestershire
'Valley with camps and a market' *Anglo-Saxon*
Population: 2062 *Market:* suspended

Chichester's Market Cross, built in 1501, lies midway in style between the earlier, plain market cross (see Grantham) and later elaborate structures (see Wymondham).

The many 'Chippings' and 'Cheaps' in English town and street names all translate as 'market'. Appropriately, the beautiful seventeenth-century Market Hall is one of Chipping Campden's outstanding pieces of architecture, together with its Perpendicular 'wool' church.

Ely, Cambridgeshire
'Eel district' *Anglo-Saxon*
Population: 10,268 *Cattle market:* Thursday
Although Ely ceased to be an island two centuries ago when the surrounding Fens were drained, it still bears the name of Isle of Ely, and stands out in the surrounding flatland crowned, almost top-heavily, by its stunning cathedral.

Godalming, Surrey
'Godhelm's people' *Anglo-Saxon*
Population: 18,209 *Market:* Friday
The charming little 'pepper pot' or Town Hall with its clock and cupola, built in 1814, gives distinction to the crowded High Street. Peter the Great stayed at the King's Arms. In 1750 Godalming was an important centre of the clothing industry and the largest town in the county.

Helston, Cornwall

'Farm by the old court' *Cornish/Anglo-Saxon*
Population: 10,741 *Market:* Saturday
Cattle: Monday

The famous Furry (or floral) Dance, held in May, is still a genuine local festival despite the crowds it attracts. It is a celebration of the fact that no harm befell the town when a dragon toppled a boulder onto it. The old Butter Market is now a mining museum, reminiscent of the time when this was a stannary town.

Henley-on-Thames, Oxfordshire

'High wood' *Anglo-Saxon*
Population: 10,976 *Market:* Thursday

Beautifully situated among wooded hills, Henley's picturesque eighteenth-century bridge spans a wide curve of the Thames. The Regatta has made the town famous, but the town centre is an architectural gem with splendid inns: the Red Lion has seen its share of personalities, Charles II among them.

Hertford, Hertfordshire

'Stag ford' *Anglo-Saxon*
Population: 20,760 *Market:* Saturday

Situated at the meeting place of three rivers – the Lea, the Rib and the Beane – this old county town contains a number of attractive buildings from Jacobean to Georgian times. The fifteenth-century gatehouse is all that remains of the Norman castle, a childhood home of Elizabeth I. At the centre of the town are the famous Bluecoat School and Lombard House, the home of Judge Sir Henry Chauncy who held the last witchcraft trial in England.

Huntingdon, Cambridgeshire

'Huntsman's hill' *Anglo-Saxon*
Population: 17,467 *Market:* Saturday

By the end of the tenth century a market and a mint had been established here, and the town grew in prosperity until the Black Death decimated its population. But it survived and was again a substantial market town by the eighteenth century when the impressive Town Hall was built. Oliver Cromwell was born here, and both he and Samuel Pepys attended the grammar school, now a museum devoted to Cromwell. Of the many fine inns The George is notable for its picturesque coaching yard. The town is linked to Godmanchester by the finest medieval bridge in the country.

The Furry Dance, Helston, which takes place in May. 'Furry' is probably a corruption of 'floral'.

The Regatta, for which Henley is famous, was first held in 1839. The bridge provides a superb grandstand.

Market Harborough, Leicestershire

'Flock hill' *Anglo-Saxon*
Population: 15,934 *Market:* Saturday
Cattle: Tuesday

The market place is still the heart of the town to which it gave its name. Look for the old grammar school which was originally the Butter Market, following the usual design of an upper chamber on stilts.

Melton Mowbray, Leicestershire

'Melton's middle farm' *Anglo-Saxon/French*
Population: 23,554 *Market:* Saturday
Cattle: Tuesday

Melton Mowbray's famous pork pies are still served at the local inns, and Stilton cheese originated here too. Also typical of the area are the superb alabaster carvings, which can be seen in the Church of St Mary.

*Windsor High Street, seen through the arches
of Sir Christopher Wren's Guildhall.*

Newbury, Berkshire

'New fort' *Anglo-Saxon*
Population: 26,396 *Market:* Thursday, Saturday
'Jack O'Newbury', the name of innumerable pubs all over England, commemorates England's first great manufacturer, John Winchcombe, who set up an immense weaving factory here in the fifteenth century. Part of his house survives, as does the ancient Cloth Hall, now a museum.

Okehampton, Devon

'Farm on the swift river' *Britannic/Anglo-Saxon*
Population: 4,181 *Market:* Saturday
The dual origin of the place name indicates the town's extreme age but, physically, it is of Norman foundation. The seventeenth-century town hall reverses the usual trend, having been originally a private house.

Oundle, Northamptonshire

'Undivided people' *Anglo-Saxon*
Population: 3290 *Market:* Thursday
The famous school, inevitably, dominates Oundle, but there are some delightful stone buildings, notably the church, the almshouses and the beautiful Talbot Inn, reminiscent of the George and Pilgrim at Glastonbury though two centuries later. It contains an oak staircase from the now dismantled Fotheringhay Castle.

Stratford-upon-Avon, Warwickshire

'Fort over the Roman road over the river'
Anglo-Saxon
Population: 20,858 *Market:* Friday
Cattle: Tuesday
Here are three distinct towns in one: scholar's haven, tourist's delight, and a gem of a Midland town, rich in vernacular architecture, sturdily going about its affairs.

Windsor, Berkshire

'Bank with a winch' *Anglo-Saxon*
Population: 28,330 *Market:* Saturday
This Thames-side town, dominated by its royal castle, still has a life of its own. Delightful houses off the High Street in Church Lane mark the site of the ancient market. Wren gave the finishing touches to the Guildhall, including the enigmatic columns which support nothing.

BIBLIOGRAPHY

NOTHING better illustrates the English indifference to their urban history than the low standard of official guide books. Few of the historic towns featured here have guides worthy of them. In some cases there is no guide book at all; in many, the book is simply a medium for local advertisements interspersed with ill-digested chunks of history and smudgy photographs. This lack is all the more surprising and depressing considering that English antiquaries have been happily burrowing into the histories of their towns for the past 200 years or more. Some of their results are slowly seeing the light in more modern readable form, but in most cases the visitor to a given town who wants to go a little further into its history will have to visit the local public library. Yet it is only fair to notice the exceptions that have substantially helped in the writing of this book. They include Cirencester (its Corinium Museum guide is outstanding), Ledbury (with an excellent town trail), Ripon (the Civic Society has produced some excellent guides), Thaxted, Bradford, Ludlow, and, of course, Marshfield, its guide lovingly produced by the local Women's Institute.

Local history on a national scale is, happily, in far better shape as a result of a remarkable renaissance. Barely a generation ago, 'local' history was myopically and contemptuously ignored in favour of 'national' history, oblivious to the fact that all history is local to somebody. Town studies in particular were largely the province of the antiquary and the dabbler, with occasional specialized forays from an academic. The swing of the pendulum over the past two decades, however, has seen urban studies emerging to enjoy the kind of glamour that attended popular archaeology in the 1950s. What follows here is a small selection of authoritative, but highly readable works which should extend and deepen the necessarily brief entries in the present book.

Historic works

Fiennes, Celia, *The Illustrated Journeys 1685–c.1712*, edited by Christopher Morris, Webb & Bower, 1982.

Defoe, Daniel, *A Tour through the Whole Island of Great Britain*, introduction by G.D.H.Cole, Peter Davies, 1927.

Leland, John, *The Itinerary 1535–1543*, edited by Lucy Toulmin Smith, Bell & Hyman, 1907.

Beginning with Leland's tours in the 1530s and ending with Defoe's in the 1730s, these three books together give a bird's eye picture of English town development just before the onslaught of the Industrial Revolution.

Contemporary works

Ashton, Michael and Bond, James, *The Landscape of Towns*, J.M.Dent & Sons, 1976. This study deduces the history of towns from their shape: excellent town plans.

Clifton-Taylor, Alex, *Six English Towns*, and *Six More English Towns*, both BBC publications, 1978 and 1981 respectively. Based on the television series, these publications deduce the history of towns from their architecture.

Hoskins, W.G., *Local History in England*, Longman, 1972. Where to look for what, and why: an invaluable handbook.

Pevsner, Nikolaus (and others), *The Buildings of England*, Penguin, various dates. The indispensable Pevsner: an architectural survey arranged by counties. Mostly a catalogue of facts but enlivened by quirky judgements.

Platt, Colin, *The English Medieval Town*, Granada, 1976. A deduction of the history of towns from archaeology.

ACKNOWLEDGMENTS

Illustrations have been reproduced by kind permission of the following:

Aerofilms Ltd: 37, 41, 62 above, 94, 102, 130
John Bethell: 23, 52–3, 58–9, 60, 61, 97, 148
Bodleian Library, Oxford: 150 (Ms. Gough Liturg. 7 f.10)
Janet and Colin Bord: 9, 68 left, 109
Local History Collection, Boston Library: 12
British Tourist Authority: 10, 14, 15 above, 20, 22 left and right, 25 left and right, 27, 32 below, 34, 66, 73 below, 79, 93, 100 above, 124, 131, 134, 138 above
J. Allan Cash Ltd: 44, 45, 69, 95, 142
Russell Chamberlin: 21, 35 below, 80, 138 below
Cliffe Bonfire Society Ltd: 42 (photo Jim Etherington)
Dr Zeta Eastes: 70 above and below
Derek Forss: 65, 122, 123
Fotobank International Colour Library Ltd: 56 above, 104, 115, 126 right
Fotobank International Colour Library Ltd/English Tourist Board: 2, 11, 17 below, 35 above, 38, 38–9, 49 above, 110, 111, 132, 133, 143
Hewitts (Knutsford) Ltd: 64
Neil Holmes: 48, 74 left, 76–7, 84 left and right, 86, 88 left and right, 89, 92, 96, 99, 100 below, 101, 105, 106, 107, 116, 117, 125
International Photobank: 19, 32 above, 33
Judges Postcards Ltd, Hastings: 57 left and right

Rick Kemp: 13
A. F. Kersting: 15 below, 18, 26 left and right, 28, 36, 43, 49 below, 75, 78, 83, 90, 91, 98, 113, 135, 136, 145
Keswick Museum: 119 right (photo W. P. Haworth)
Peter Lewis: 29, 30
Mansell Collection: 63
Nick Meers: endpapers
National Portrait Gallery: 118
Susan Nichols: 4, 72, 73 above, 129 right, 139
Romney, Hythe and Dymchurch Light Railway Company: 40 right
Kenneth Scowen: 40 left, 74 right
Sefton Photo Library: 55, 56 below, 68 right
Local History Museum, Shaftesbury: 51
Brian Shuel: 71
Edwin Smith: 16, 17 above, 67, 81, 82, 87, 103 left and right, 108 left, 112, 140
Swanston Graphics: 7
Jeffery W. Whitelaw: 24, 54 left and right, 62 below, 108 right, 144
Derek G. Widdicombe: 31 (photo Noel Habgood), 46, 47 (photo Noel Habgood), 50 (photo Noel Habgood), 114, 120–1, 126 left, 127 left and right, 128–9, 141 (photo Noel Habgood), 146 (photo Frieda Stanbury), 147
Woodmansterne Publications Ltd: 85, 119 left (photos Nicholas Servian)

*An early calendar, c. 1500, showing a market scene
in which a cattle auction is
in progress.*

INDEX

Page numbers in *italic* type indicate illustrations.

151